3

Moses Basket

My pen hesitates

What can I say?

I wonder where you are

I wonder what you're doing

Have you forgotten?

I haven't.

I can't.

It lies beside me in my bed.

I sleep with my head in my pillow

to escape pictures of you.

You have burned the cradle,

broken into the sanctuary where one day

my child will sleep, so softly breathing.

You have torn down its walls,

severed the strength,

destroyed the protection it gives.

Men do not know it but

a woman's body can have two hearts:

One a beating muscle the size of a fist

The other a silent chamber that crouches deep in her belly

softly biding its time, just in case.

I want to see you dead,

lying, so pathetic, in an unmarked grave.

The way you have left me.

I hate you for what you have done,

and I hate the hatred you have bred in me.

You have killed something.

You have killed my baby.

Because of you it will sense the sadness inside its mother

Because of you it will hurt, my child.

Because of you I can't protect it, my child.

There, in that sacred place.

So let me tear my body to pieces,

and burn everything you have ever touched,

destroy everything you have ever gazed upon.

Because of you everything has turned to evil

Therefore

I am evil?

No. But full of this screaming hatred

That wants to see you gone from memory

out of sight,

out of thoughts that creep into

the lonely peace of solitude.

Solitude. One year, one hundred, it's all the same.

Solitude. Ha! The word is a joke.

All words are a joke.

What do they have to do

with the human mind?

with human suffering?

They are shapes and sounds and music

to ease the listener's ear

concealing a hideous truth.

They lie.

And now the memory is all I have.

I look at myself and I see your disease

You, you are a work of pure evil and

Nature does not trust you

Nature did not create you - *could not* have created you -

because when I am alone I can see that everything

is colour and Life!

and Life is everything that is Beauty.

But at night I look at the Moon and I see how

She reflects everything that we have destroyed.

People are what make the world an unsafe place.

People, persons, power. You.

Funny.

I am writing this on a religious day

and even today I am thinking of you

Christ, memory can be a bitch.

It never sleeps.

Plucks away at the flesh,

eats me alive.

Who said 'my body is a temple'?

They lied to me.

My body it is not so Holy now -

I can't stand to touch it.

And the Devil has entered it.

anonymous

cutting

cropped short feels

like exhalation:

punk sigh of right.

something about

long hair

reminds me

of tears

all down the front,

a friend

after the first time,

before she cut it off

and bought new boots,

grew tall. then

it happened again

times two.

reminds me of tangled

feminine juices

with guilt

crystallizing down

phone lines,

after other friends

cut their hair,

forty-third man walks.

calls from the girl

who became a doctor,

said she would pay

with her soul to rub off

these couple of scars

by next tuesday week.

times

for her voice

to find succour

by echolocation,

i would worry

thumbs into crosses

for her utility bills,

student loans,

fret in quiet

for a night

nine years ago.

sometimes fall asleep,

ear to receiver,

wanting to show her

someone was there

when louisiana got dark.

long hair reminds me

of all my "her"s.

secrets of the majority,

walking open into

bitumen cities.

sometimes long hair

makes anger rise in tresses.

   mess. bibless.

   bless.

Khairani Barokka

Ragging

It was difficult to know
Which cloth to suffocate
The wall of his memory
With: the pinstripe shirt
In *carnevale* colours,
That sweater with the
Insignia of an
Unnecessary bar
Bingo team.

He'd wanted the kitchen
Painted blood orange,
Noting the exact shade
Of pulse that flurried
To her lip when she bit it.

Dipped in smart
Smokey tones,
His socks, all fifteen
Left in the drawers,
Mismatched and crumpled,
Doused with her hands
In buckets of pigment,
Applied to every surface

That threatened to
Amount to trigger.
The act, she consciously
Thought, felt like larvicide.

She could never sell
The house otherwise,
In case another woman
Was prone to biting
The outside of her mouth
When inflamed, driven
To pressure on the skin,
The changing of one's
Own tautness,
Reddened cries gone

To the ends of all rope.

Khairani Barokka

A goose and fishes.

I never asked you
What the fuck you thought you were doing
When you goosed me
In the hallway,
While we were watching
The new fish.
A shoal of neons,
Darting through the water weed,
Moving as one,
As you slid your hand
Across my bum
And touched my vagina
With your middle finger
And we both pretended that it didn't happen
Even while it was happening
We both pretended
That it was a mistake
But it wasn't.
You didn't mistake me for my mother
And you knew it wasn't right
And something in me curdled
Because it was what I had been expecting.
In my thirties
I told you, vaguely

What I believed the other man with the fish,

The man next door, had done to me

And you said, "I'm not surprised"

And turned away.

Ali Bee

Dancing forward.

When I was a child,

I danced forward,

Forever open to the future.

You waltzed me

Into a corner,

With your adult hands

And showed me darkness,

Through your eyes.

Today,

Thirty years later,

I burned the toy you gave me,

Bribery for silence.

I watched, as,

Lit by bright clean flames,

It shrivelled, till it resembled

Nothing more

Than the piece

Of shit it was.

My friends hugged me

And I thought,

Look at me, again

I'm dancing forward.

Ali Bee

Fish Man.

He is the fish man.

Cold eyes and sallow skin.

He keeps his secrets

Behind his eyes,

As he keeps his fish

Behind glass.

Everybody thinks he is

A nice man.

He is the fish man.

He tells me I must keep

A secret too,

For cold eyed fish men

Can make bad things happen

To the families

Of little girls who tell

And anyway

Didn't he give me

A lovely present

He is the fish man.

He slides, eel like

Into my memory,

When a gesture,

Or a feature,

Or cold, ice eyes,

Remind me

He is the fish man.

And now he swims with me

Always.

Ali Bee

It must be the orange Juice

There could be no other explanation

For the pain

In my little girl body.

Not understanding why it hurt so much

I cried.

I need a wee,

It hurts

But I need a wee,

But it hurts.

And then the medicine

Would make it better,

But soon it would come back.

It must be the orange juice

Said the doctor,

Agreed my mum

And sure enough stopping the orange juice

Stopped the pain.

Nobody noticed

That we had new neighbours

At the same time.

Ali Bee

Still I rage

Taught to be compliant,

By neighbour,

By parent's friend's brother,

By daddy's 'airport books',

Where women always

Opened their legs and enjoyed,

No matter who,

No matter what,

No matter where

I raged and ate (anything, everything)

I raged and was fucked (like this, like that)

I raged and was beaten (safe word, no words)

I raged and you laughed (daddy, my daddy)

I raged and wept

And weep,

But still, I raged

And rage, still.

Ali Bee

We are all the caged bear.

We are all the caged bear,

The circus animal,

The slave.

Kept compliant

With sugared words,

The whip,

Or hopes of small freedoms.

We are all the

Actors of our lives,

Inventing each moment,

Living our novel,

Trying for truth.

Never knowing what comes

From the real us

Or the trained animal,

Face painted, costumed,

Body distorted

Seeking prizes for

A trick well performed.

Ali Bee

Running Scared

I saw what happened
When you gave your heart
To another woman,
When you opened yourself
With pride
And honesty.
I saw what happened
When your circle
Turned their backs,
Turned away their faces,
Cold shouldered you
While you held out your hands
In supplication
And the masked men
Medicated you.
I saw what happened
When I visited you
And you told me they
Drugged you,
Electrocuted you,
Battered you into obedience.
I saw what happened
And I am ashamed.
I ran,

I also turned my back

And pretended there was

Nothing wrong

When they sent you home

To the life they invented for you,

Where housework and ironing

Were key

And you moved in with a man

Who didn't mind you were a lesbian

Or so you told me.

So, running scared

I ignored you when you told me

You loved me

And pretended

I didn't love you back.

I think of you often

And wonder

If you're still alive

I wonder if you've

Found yourself again

Under the pain

I look for you

In faces that pass

And wish and hope

That you did.

Ali Bee

I'm sorry for being a dick

I'm sorry for being a dick,

I just can't control it you see,

It's the way I was raised

And you'd be amazed

How you women all oppress me.

I'm sorry for being a dick,

Saying sorry should make it ok,

It wipes it all out,

You shouldn't have any doubt,

Just believe every word that I say.

I'm sorry for being a dick,

But it's really your fault, you're so slow.

You should keep your mouth shut,

No ifs, ands or buts,

You belong here, I won't let you go.

I'm sorry for being a dick

But I own you, you're mine, don't you know.

Now get yourself straight,

This is love, never hate,

With some make up the bruises won't show.

I'm sorry for being a dick,

But you married me, so it's my right.

You should just love me back

And we'd be back on track,

Now roll over, I'm asking polite.

I'm sorry for being a dick,

But she asked for it man, can't you see.

I'd had all I could take,

Her death was a mistake,

You don't want to put handcuffs on me.

Ali Bee

Did we do well, my darling girls.

For the young women involved in 'antifeminism'

Did we do well, my darling girls?

Did we really do well?

We grew you up to be straight and strong,

To do your best and know right from wrong,

But we grew you in this awful world,

A world that's hard and tough for girls

And part of your strength was to take it,

To take it and make it ok.

But it's not ok my darling girls

In this fucked up, muddled up, mixed up world

And it's not ok to be always poor

And expect the bailiffs at your door

And it's not alright for a man to treat

You as if your nothing and then to cheat

And it's not alright to be punched and beat

And it's not ok for the man on the street

To lick his lips as if you're meat,

To have you primp and have you preen

When your inner self is never seen

And you're invisible.

Did we do well my darling girls?

Did we really do well?

When we kept from you, the truth of the world,

That the world's not safe for a woman or girl,

That men will kill and rape and maim

And that most of them are much the same,

Hooked on porn and killing games,

They'll steal your soul but give you their names

And never show an ounce of shame

But say our oppressions are all the same

And really women are to blame

For their rapes and deaths. They make it plain

That they hate us.

Did we do well my darling girls?

Did we really do well?

When we told you that your source of pride

Was not something that came from deep inside,

But your looks, your weight and being a bride

And your wisdom and knowledge you learned to hide,

While your spirit dimmed, curled up and died.

For we've learned to be slaves so very well,

To keep the secrets and not to tell,

To flatter the masters, believe it's real,

No matter what our hearts may feel.

We'll box up our doubts, behind cold steel

And shout down our sisters with jealous zeal.

We'll throw to the sharks a tasty meal

And convince ourselves that we got the best deal,

To keep us safe.

I don't know the answers, my darling girls,

But I know what's wrong and what's right

And I know some women, courageous women

Who'll stand their ground and fight.

They'll speak their truth, they'll stand their ground,

Their heads held high, their courage found

And they fight for you and they fight for me

And they light the way so that we can see

How to be the best that we can be,

So women and girls can someday be free.

Yet we weep for all the wasted years,

The wasted lives, so many tears,

But at last when all the tears are gone

And we've learned in ourselves, how to be strong,

We battle on.

song lyrics by Ali Bee

The Illusion of being in control.

This ball gagged life

Is not what you supposed

And even if you hold the whip

The rules are male imposed.

This ball gagged life,

You've wandered through it, mute,

Insisting you're a rebel

Whilst trying to look cute.

This ball gagged life,

You'll never be a winner

The race is fixed, you'll only be

A virgin or a sinner.

This ball gagged life,

Your body's not your own

You'll do as you are bid,

You'll do as you are shown.

This ball gagged life,

While you heave against the chains,

No wonder you are crazy,

No wonder you're in pain.

This ball gagged life,

How much violence can we take?

How much rape and murder

Must we have before we wake?

This ball gagged life,

Filled with ever growing mourning

While the masters murder us.

Life shouldn't need a trigger warning.

Ali Bee

She Said. He Said

I said you only knew me
In reverse
As the absence of the there
The othering a daily chore

You said I was sensitive
Too fragile
Too quick to judge
Too emotional

I said I wasn't born that way
The world had forced me so
Had painted me pink and white
And chopped up the easel

You said I was full of hate
Full of anger
Full of shit
Twisting your words

I said I did hate
And hate is learned
When all that you are is hated
Try dialling down that righteous anger

You said it wasn't so

It wasn't universal hatred

It wasn't all men

It wasn't

I looked you in the eye

And dared you

To stare right back

And say that with a straight face

You could not.

I'll give you that.

Catharine Brockhurst

Ms World

Ms World clacks her heels
Trit-trot, click-clack
Her ankles fail
To carry the weight
Of the world

Ms world burns her soles
On the scalding glass
Of sand heated
By a sun too large
To hide from

Ms world binds her toes
And watches as the stumps
Bring joy and passion
To the eyes of the men
Staring through peepholes

Ms World straps her breasts down
Pretending they never arrived

Ms World injects her breasts with liquid sand
Her skin a coating, a gritty mix inside

Ms World hides her breasts beneath cloth
The child attached hidden too

Ms world bares her breasts
To the army and guns facing her down

Ms World chops her breasts from her form
Avoiding the death they'll bring

Ms World worships her breasts
The only way to save her starving child

Ms World hates herself
Ms World denies herself
Ms World attacks herself
Ms world frightens herself
Ms world questions herself

In a world not built for her
Not designed for her
Where she isn't catered for
Or heard
Ms world is the afterthought

Catharine Brockhurst

The Beautiful Song

The beautiful song
Wrestled in my chest
Playing to burst free
Clear rivers of silver
Threading through
Every verse

The beautiful song
Out in the open
A duet
Sung by one
Gold seas stitched through
Carrying us adrift

Our beautiful song
Out among the stars
Carried to the airless ends
Sung to me
Pitch navy velvet
Comforting us home

Catharine Brockhurst

See the Little Princess

Out she erupted

Kicking and screaming

Boiled lobster

Singing on the hob

A slate free of chalk

Until out came the brush

Dipped in pink

Cotton candy

Out came the ribbons

And hearts

And the sugar

And spice

And the chains

And the war paint

And the wires

And the points

Out came the drugs

And gag

The Ropes

And Camera

See the little princess
Watch her grow
See her sparkle
Watch her glow

See the little princess
Ancient now
See her finished
And take her bow

See the little princesses
Ever on show
Pink on pink
Perfect in a row

Catharine Brockhurst

A Better Man

I tried

You said

To be a better man

I did what I could

I did my fair share

Sat on a seesaw

Trimmed with velvet

Dripping in honey

Tipped to the heavy

I tried

You said

To be a better man

To level a playing field

Riddled with potholes

That you had a map for

And a shovel and terf

But the holes stayed unfilled

You just followed your map

I tried

You said

To be a better man

To carry the burden

Of a job you chose

Of a life you chose

Of a wife you chose

Of a path you chose

Where anything goes

Where your clothes are

Yours

And your words are

Yours

And your home is

Yours

And your food is

Yours

And your body is

Yours

Your choices yours

I tried

You said

To be a better man

While the other men

They tried too

All trying

So hard

With gentle eyes

And sincere words

And hipster beards

Men of action

Men in space

Men splitting atoms

Men cloning sheep

Men cheating death

Men with the will

To even-steven the world?

They're still trying

Oh so very hard

They must be shattered

Catharine Brockhurst

Spent

It started with the golden

With the bubbles cut with acid

With the burn and the bite

With the sickly sweet

The confused fumblings

The morning rumblings

A barely there faze

And a mustard heat haze

Then the golden turned

The silver replaced

The liquid alloy

Hitting every surface

Down to the fingernails

Down to the quick

The whole lemon

Stuck in a throat

Oozing citric

From pores made to breathe

Clogged with a hurt

That dulls

With the shot

Through the chest

And the pints of pain
Dousing a raging fire

The self medication
Of the liar
Telling tales to oneself
In the long old nights
And the endless mornings
The lining failing
The skin falling away
The reasons repeated

As a mantra
The lie you repeat
In the hope of belief
The partner you have to leave
The child you must abandon
I'm your pill and your poison
Your start and your end
A bottomless well to nowhere

Put out my fire
With a run through the bitter
A biting wind to clear
The fear

Kick at the dying embers

With a love for the now

For the open and solemn

For the real and sincere

Catharine Brockhurst

Little Ripples

I compared
Oh and measured
No-one spared
No-one treasured

Every sound I ever heard
Seldom trilled Only grated
A deadened word
Lonely, hated

Nighttime caught me
A crooked trap
Bad dreams sought me
For their lap

I was bitter dark, a void
I was hollow and obtuse
I was nasty, paranoid
Thriving in abuse

But little ripples jollied me
To count another way
Setting follies fancy free
Another slate cleaned day

The echoes sit a way on top
They always have their place
And now a bumper crop
I see it in your face

A new and humble line
Is told from time to time
It's bold in depth but fine
And simple yet sublime

To try and try again
To be the better man
To swallow all that pain
And know you did, You can

I compared
Oh and measured
No-one spared
No-one treasured

But try and try again
To be the better man
To swallow all that pain
And know you did, You can

Catharine Brockhurst

To be full and free

What if

You didn't have to be beautiful

What if

You just were

Your emerald

Sapphire and

Cats eye

What if you knew

That the folds of silk

And sand

And warm toffee

Were all that mattered

The feel and the taste

The joy

Of the breath in and out

What if those years

Spent

Leaving you spent

The counting and

Deducting

The shrinking

And control

What if

You could claim them back

For your mother

And your daughter

And you

What if you could

Use that time

To build and strengthen

Dance and sing

Hold and love

Learn and live

What if

We all did that

Every woman

Our world would

And should

Be full

And free

Catharine Brockhurst

Queens of the mountain

I couldn't get to The Mountain

So you fearlessly brought it to me

Placed me at its foot

And said climb

You showed me where

And how

You pointed at who

And what I must do

My footing never sure

You never explained why

The reason for the journey

You wouldn't tell me why

Why the mountain

Why the need for the mountain pass

Why the need for counsel

Why the need for you

I scaled midway up

Had an ariel view

And I found the answer

Staring down to the upturned faces

All battling with the rock

Some on ledges

Others tumbling down

The first steps always guided

While the whirling blades

Were abseiling them in

Dropping those men

Onto the summit

Landing atop surveying us

While we climbed and climbed

With barely a toehold to start

Exhaustion taking us at the peak

Catharine Brockhurst

Still Counting

I put one bare foot in front of the other

The blades damp, reaching up

Between my toes

The trickles over the tops of my feet

Cooling

The breeze on my bare skin

Taking a layer off

Peeling away the dirt

And the time

Washing off your evil, mundane work

Your everyday behaviour

Your daily beatings

You, the perfect father

You, the loving husband

You, who broke me

Staring up the skies join the rooftops

Those tiled lids balancing

On a solid base

Housing all manner of ills

I float a little

Feel a dull buzzing

Then I rise

Seeing myself laid out on a ground

A peace falling

And my goodbyes are made

I fly higher

Over the London Eye

The buildings filled with men

Counting beans

Instead of us

They should be counting us

Summing our parts to a total

But higher and higher I climb

The reds and golds stunning me

Racing now I'm gone

Free on the wind

Catharine Brockhurst

The Shadow

In the half light

You could be mistaken

For anything other

Than the person you are

The shadows hiding

The budding bruises

The dusk masking

The sodden sheets

Those dreams

Where you run

But stay on one spot

You scream

But your vocal cords

Have been cut

You claw at the sides

But stay in the well

Are a waking nightmare

An every day life you live

Those roundabouts

You spun on

Air through hair

Face upturned

Where you'd gather speed

Were the last

Real time

When you felt alive

Too many decades ago

Catharine Brockhurst

The Denounced

Sat in a pod

Or at a desk

A sofa

A lawn

Lying in bed

You scan with your code

And your algorithms of shame

Eyeballing for the sleights

The choice keywords

Juicy tidbits to wave under

The noses of your allies

Tracking

The allegiances formed

Through shared experiences

And you frighten

Condemn and denounce

These keyboard "aggressors"

You are known to us

You scream

From a page backlit

And we are watching you

Looking at your language

Looking for your hate

Avoid these scum

You warn

While actively searching them out

These women

With voices

These questioning

Inquisitive women

These thinking

Breathing

Challenging

Women

Reducing them to sound bites

Stereotypes

Privileged and hated

Ostracised

For expressing opinions

For naming their oppression

For questioning

For speaking

Catharine Brockhurst

Those Days

You talk of those days
When they'd burn us at the stake
When they'd bridle us
The Scolds

You talk of those days
When they'd sterilise the unmarried
Force feed the challenging
Lock up the hysterical

You talk and talk and talk
Without listening
Can't you hear
The screaming

It's deafening
The white noise you hear
Is crystal clear
To those who choose to listen

Those days are these days
That time is now
The burning
And the bridles

The detention centres

The sedation

The medication

The sterilisation

The force

Blunt trauma

Are you listening

Can't you hear

Catharine Brockhurst

The Metal Yard

Coat me in gold leaf

The edible kind

For I am consumable

Unwrap me

And devour

Sprinkle me with silver sugar balls

That live atop cakes

For I am decorative

A luxury

A bad habit

Brush me with bronze

Burnish me in steel

Watch my copper oxidise

And my iron rust

As I stand out facing the storm

Wrap me in arms

Held at their length

Breathe in my collarbones

And swallow my heartbeat

A metronome to count on

Lift me and swing me

Sway me and move me

Convince me of a truth told

Or I'll dance far far away

Out of this metal yard

Catharine Brockhurst

The Gap in the Writing

The welcome depth in white

Pulls on the strings

Tugging until sleep bellows

And if the heart wants

What the heart wants

Why can't mine decide

It'll laugh a little

And sit back on haunches

Sprung

A potential energy

In waiting

Bound to use every fuse

It'll knowingly wreck

And strip bare

Any thoughts found wanting

Any thoughts needing answers

It'll rip apart the plans and stare

Into a gap in the writing

Where the buzzwords and cliches live

Where the reality gets ignored

And the expectations

Take over

And force a frogmarch

Down a path never asked for

So I'll live a lifetime

In a foggy phase

With no directions

Or decisions made

And I'll play at the role

Agreed by everyone but me

Catharine Brockhurst

How do you have sex?

How do you do it without a …
Do you just kiss? Will you kiss for us?

What if every adult got this interrogation,
hi, great to meet you, are you into *Fifty Shades*?
Have you got the time love? Who goes on top?

And of course you're interested
you're a twelve year old East London black boy
or a twenty something, Moroccan, without papers
who sleeps on a couch in a London squat
or a random man on a bus or a train who just won't
shut up and somehow it came up,
perhaps I turned you down when you offered
to lick my ass crack on public transport
or maybe my butch girlfriend gave it away
standing in the doorway when I asked you
to please stop throwing crab apples at me

Or you shouted across the plane aisle
Oi ginger! Oi bitch! It's OK for you,
you can get any man you want

But what I can't get

is away from any man I don't want

conducting a conversation with me like

I'm a hole

and they're the power tip that will fit

and everybody tells you this plug works

for every socket, so you take it home, try it

from small to large but you can't get a connection

so you bring it back to the shop and the man

has that look, the you didn't try it properly look,

you just need me to show you how its done, look.

I'm a cave woman, discovering

if you rub the right two stones together

you get fire, I've got ten of what he's got

I can go as long and hard as you like

and I know there's no such thing as a

universal changer.

Cat Brogan

Twenty Four

Eighteen then, forty two now -

That makes twenty four years.

My waist at eighteen was thirty -

I still had puppy fat – my measurement

At twenty four, twenty three

And now at forty two, I record a thirty five.

I learned to eat again but

The price of that was padding.

Twenty four years since you failed

In your claim of ownership -

Twenty four years since

I won and you lost – if winning is

What it means to allocate your years

In sections, twelve in each then

Divided out again into fours.

There are seven days in a week

And every one of those days

Is filled at some point

With a thought

Of you.

Jane Burn

No wonder I'm fat

I seemed to be always wearing his hands.
Thumb and finger on my earlobe, squeezing
a bit too hard – *why were you talking to him?*
You were seen. Hand moves under my hair,
finds the roots, discreetly pulls. *They watch,*
you know. My friends, they tell me everything.

People think nothing of it - just some bloke,
seeing to his lass. *Got your 'ands full there mate –*
collusion winks across the room, eyes on my breasts
in this tight little dress. Close to my ear - *I could*
have killed you, you know. Taken you up the fields
where nobody would see. I nearly did.

This is what pretty gets you – this, I learn is what
comes
of slinking in velour. I used to dance in high heels.
My throat feels like a paper cup under his circlet.
Tears trigger his tender protection; *now then.*
Don't spoil your face. Erection against my thigh,
knee between mine, bus shelter whines

behind my back. *Don't do it again.*

Jane Burn

66

I am clean

My thoughts chunked in porcelain shapes - a tea cup, spatchcocked
on the floor marks where I lost my concentration. I was mouthing
milk and sugar when it came to me again; bank-burst, rinsing round
my temples, rushing in my ears; I sandbag with my hands.

Stilettos too big for my feet, a kid in her mother's shoes, crawling pubs,
brimmed with booze. I love the dancing; sing out loud to Bronski Beat.
Streets, loud with knee-deep people dancing on Billie-Jean pavements;
gold chains, Pepe Jeans. A tunnel of sound, lights smeared in yellow
through dark – car windows down – *where you goin'?* As if!

Stones at my bedroom window, *tap, tap.* My eyes grit, mouth a rat's nest –
tap. Him on the kerb. *I just want to talk*, he smiles; a curl that is more thin line.
A light flicks on next door - a curtain twitches. I open the door, his hand

spans the gap. My heart is high. *I just want to talk.* Walking behind me

up the stairs, I can hear his footsteps weighted with breath.

I open my eyes; he is stroking my hair. *There*, he says, cold as dawn. Smears,

crisp like a burn graft, filming my thigh. I think of my favourite things – pencils,

ponies. That painting I love, the Valpincon Bather; wonder if one day, I could

paint like that. Her neck, arched like a Camargue mare turned to scent the water –

hair, bound in twisted wrapping, lest it spill, mar the pastel fleshing of her back.

A hand that rubs the covering of white sheets, perhaps to reassure them

I am clean. I am clean.

Jane Burn

'You Should Be Afraid, He Says'

You should be scared, he says –

You should be scared, he says you should carry a weapon or only
things that can become a weapon at a moment's notice –
your keys should not just be keys your jewellery not just
ornament –
you should be scared and everything on your person should
remind you of that fear –
the world is dark and it will be darker still with the weight of its
violence carried on your hip in the bag that is not a bag but a
vault –
remember this violence that was this violence that is this
violence that will be - you are at its centre –
what he does not say is –
You should be scared because if you are not then the violence
turns elsewhere - because if it does then he cannot say that there
is nothing to be scared of; that he has never felt unsafe.

Stephani Campisi

69

She laughs at his jokes

It is winter (although it could be any season) and a woman –

with a generous and unearned laugh –

donates her soul sets herself bare gives her warming cape of self

to the man she walks with to wear over his mantle of ego –

he is warm and masculine with his layers of comfort as she

shivers, stripped of her own fabric.

Stephani Campisi

The Awakening

Drifting, sleeping, eyes unopened
Moving slowly through the torrents
Suspended in a timeless place
Waiting for...The Awakening

Numbness, blackness, a living façade
Hiding a pain, guarding the heart
Floating beneath or above the alive
Nearing...The Awakening

Stirring, tingling, the shroud is lifting
Examination reveals the falseness
Shifting fault, revelatory moment
Then begins -The Awakening

Anguish, grief, pain abounding
Poise morphs into shame
Reality becomes a burden intolerable
I am Awake

Natalie Collins

An almost resolution

An almost resolution, before
An absolute anomaly today
My posture would deceive
That which my heart does portray

Self belief lost one moment
Shame surfacing, overtaking
A child in an adult's body
Innocence defiled, I am breaking

Natalie Collins

Beauty so real

Beauty so real
Beauty so true
Beauty I feel
Since I left you

Constant put downs
No real love
Couldn't talk about it
To even God above

Hope all gone
Accepted my fate
Until that night
I saw your worst trait

Slapping me, raping me
Breaking me up
Never did I think
That'd be what it took

I'm in a good place now
With God as my guide
I can talk about it
In even God I confide

Beauty so real

Beauty so true

Beauty I feel

Since I left you

Natalie Collins

Cracks in the ceiling

I look at the ceiling seeing a small crack

I hear in the distance someone hurting a lot

I stare at the crack as it slowly creeps out

Hearing distant grunts and terrible pain

The spidery lines of the cracks are growing

I count them as the sounds grow louder

Quickly they become an uncountable amount

The sounds have dulled but their pain intensified

As plaster dust falls onto my face

Crevices, fissures and chinks open above

While the sound of hurt can no longer be quieted

As the ceiling falls in pieces smashing against my body

The man I married gets up and starts to redress

Natalie Collins

Feelings of Me

Sometimes I wonder why I'm here

Why I don't just leave or die or just be

But then I realise it's 'cause I'm yours

You wouldn't have it another way

You're not really mine

Though you aim to please

You don't really care

But you know you do

I cant make sense of myself

Don't worry,

But you won't

You care about me

But not about them

Those feelings that make me the person I am

And if I could, I'd move on

But that won't ever be

Because you're not really mine

Though you aim to please

You don't really care but you know I do

You fuck me and with me

And love me and make it

But do you care

I mean really care?

Of course you do, and don't

When it's too much

To bother with and stay waking for

You'd rather be in slumbers

So sweet and delightful

Than being a caring person of love

I know you don't mean it

And that's past your capabilities

But it'd be great if you'd think

For more than one moment

About things like my feelings

And the reason for those

The pain, it hurts me

Sometimes and always

Whenever you fuck me or with me or near me

Not that you do that

You can't anymore

The guilt is too much

It's not my pain or my scars

'Oh the scars!' you say
What are they?
You know what I mean
My feelings and needings
And wantings and hurts

But they don't matter the time has gone by
And no more confusings
And hurtings and pain
Because you are asleep now
And I am alone................

.......Good morning my love
Good morning my dear
Won't this be a nice day
And a nice year

We'll have so much fun and laughter, no needs
And those things are forgotten
What things, in deed
Nothing
Just love and niceness and

Natalie Collins

78

The grass roots grow

As the months go by
And the grass roots grow
Past the scorching sun
And the raging snow

The birthdays missed
Presents ungiven
Life goes on
No matter if you're living

Through happy days
And tears of pain
Missing the endings
And the starting again

First days of school
Uniform worn with pride
Mother, uncle, friend
No father on side

Our life has moved on
It moves further each day
In each of our memories
You're fading away

You kept your freedom

But lost your soul

You held onto your pride

But lost every goal

I pity you sometimes

Hate you never

But your part in our lives

Is lost forever

Natalie Collins

I am stupid

I am stupid

I am clumsy

A whore bag

And a cunt face

I'm an idiot

I'm useless

A fuck face

And a twat

You hate me

I piss you off

You don't care,

How I feel

I'm not a princess

I talk too much

I don't know anything

I'll never be good enough

If this is what you think,

Why do you stay with me?

Don't say it's because you love me

Because it's not from

Natalie Collins

I fall obedient

Nothing is real

I cannot feel

How do I be

If I cant see?

Emptyness consuming

Reality not resuming

I tried my best

But lost the rest

Always caring

You unsharing

Sacrifice salvation

Soul cremation

Unrealistic word

My need absurd

Only self hating

Hurt creating

At you're bading

I fall obedient

Natalie Collins

I went to a group today

I went to a group today
To learn about myself
To deal with all those things
I had put up on the shelf

I went to a group today
Full of all us victims
Different situations
All the same symptoms

I went to a group today
To make me feel better
But I felt from bad to worse
With each sentence, word and letter

Thinking about what he did to me
All the things I'm forgetting
It trying to escape from me
In what they call 'a safe setting'

They say it's ok to talk
And really good to cry
But what about if you do that
And it makes you want to die

I was getting on just fine
In that ignorance called bliss
When along comes the worksheet
And I fall into the abyss

The place that says he did it
The place where the hurt is real
Somewhere I can't pretend
Somewhere I have to feel

So I turn the worksheet over
It didn't happen to me
It's normal to be like that
That's the way that love should be

Though breathing's getting harder
And the pretence wearing thin
I get to the end of the group
And I'm still intact within

They ask me how I felt today
Nothing, cuz it's not real
So the question passes me by
And it's a relief not to feel

Natalie Collins

Why is the question

Why is the question
That always comes to mind
The problem for me,
The answer, I can't find

I want to understand you
To know you're not just bad
The belief that you're kind of good
Was all I ever had

I thought you were damaged
And that was the reason why
But I was damaged too
And I didn't make you cry

Maybe it was your bad upbringing
That made you hurt me so
But others have it just as bad
And they've never stooped so low

I thought it could've been
Because you didn't know God
You did, but chose the devil
And the evil that he had

I have realized now

There's no answer to the why

No big because

Nothing to justify

Natalie Collins

Hatred drives him

Hatred drives him
Right becomes wrong
In the world of the dominator
The weak are ruled by the strong

I wasn't chosen
For my body or mind
But for my weakness
There's no grand design

A piece of meat
There for him to take
I need sorting out
With the rules he will make

Real men take charge
Real men always fight
Sex isn't my choice
It's his 'God given' right

I like it rough
A beating always works
He knows that really
I love it when it hurts

I'm there for his pleasure

His slave without pay

He does it because

That's the 'right' way

I didn't make him do it

The reason is never me

It's not my fault

That just cannot be

It's because he believes

He's always in the right

It's because society

Tells him he's right

I am never the cause

I can't make him do it

He wants control

That's all there is to it

Natalie Collins

Want my daddy

'Want my daddy' shes says
As the tears fall
When she banged her knee
Falling off the wall

'Want my daddy' she says
As my heart breaks
Can't tell her he hurt me
Can't explain his mistakes

'Want my daddy' she says
As I cuddle her close
I didn't want this
It's not what I chose

'Daddy's not here'I say
As I try not to cry
So thankful she's not old enough
To know the reason why

Natalie Collins

Stop

Please, please stop cheating

I just want you to be mine

Please stop playing

Give me something of your time

Stop touching me that way

I don't want to do that

Stop lying, tell me the truth

Stop being such a prat

Stop isn't in your language

Its something you don't understand

If you don't get it asking

You'll just start to demand

You are so damn perverted

You dragged me down along the way

Got me to the point

'Stop!' was something I couldn't say

You pushed me till I gave in

Using manipulation and control

Made me feel it was your right

Because Id given you my soul

My silence yelled it out
As did my cries of pain
'Stop!' The unspoken plea
As you hurt me once again

Silently I screamed that word
As my eyes bulged
Quietly I whispered that word
As you yourself indulged

No need for those cries anymore
Stop is said no more
Not since I made it full stop
To you I closed the door

Full stop to your abuse
Full stop to your lies
Full stop to your cheating
And your useless alibis

Full stop to your insults
Full stop to your control
Full stop to your put downs
Full stop to you as a whole

Natalie Collins

The Bottle

There was a bottle.

It's hard to picture the bottle as it used to be,

without all its little dents and idiosyncrasies.

It was a normal bottle...

whatever that means.

He struck it

so hard that everyone thought it would break.

It hit the floor at such a speed

and the rest of the world stood

still

The flexible contours seemed to bulge

as the liquid fizzed and raged within.

Rigid, cold, self-serving and –protecting,

the threat of explosion at first contact.

They watched the bottle from a distance

or sidestepped and pretended not to see.

It was damaged now, no good to drink

and too volatile by far.

Who was surprised that the bottle "fell"?

It had been too close to the edge, they said.

Why lay blame on someone else or
make a fuss of the distant past?

One woman came into the room,
she hadn't seen the event, she didn't care.
She ripped off the lid in one swift move...
WHOOSH

It spilt out like an uncontrollable geyser,
over the room, the table, her hands.
The woman panicked, replaced the lid
and knocked the bottle again in her haste.

It lay dented and scratched,
abandoned on the floor
as – one by one –
people left the room
silently.

A hand reached out and lifted it
back onto the table, to a safe space.
She released the gas slowly, surely
and gave the time to settle.

"It's okay," she murmured patiently,

"I can clear up the mess.
My hands were sticky anyway,
and someone needs to help."

As the froth dissolved,
the liquid rose again.
It still remained in its vessel
Just calmer, stiller, more
manageable.

Where it had spilled out before,
the bottle wasn't empty.
It was full of air and other stuff
that allowed it to move and flow.

The bottle became a paradox;
different, yet still the same.
It had held together and weathered the storm
its dents easing, but scratches remained
as reminders of its

T.J. Collins

They Said

"She was drunk," they said,
"She had only herself to blame."
The voices of acceptable mitigation
drowned out the simple truth.

"She shouldn't have walked alone," they said
so many times that she began to believe.
The burden of his guilt became hers,
weighing heavy on her shoulders.

"She was asking for it," they said;
the short skirt, high heels...
Even the feminists complained
of how she succumbed to the patriarchy.

"She's just seeking attention," they said,
oblivious to the real facts.
Women lie, they're vindictive and sly,
or so we're told each day.

"She's jealous, she just wants revenge," they said.
"Nothing more than a lovers' spat."
As if his reputation was tarnished
wrongly, without cause.

"It's such a tragedy," they said.

Not her death, but his trial.

Who cares about her? She took her own life –

Another number, not a name.

T.J. Collins

Topsy Turvy

If he meant she and she were he,

how upside down the world would be.

He'd be fretting about his shape,

she'd be battling the red tape.

He'd be 'wearing a Dior gown'

or giving reporters a 'worried frown'.

She'd be praised for her success,

for film or stage or political address.

He'd be 'kind', 'loyal' or 'stunning',

she'd be a 'stalwart', 'game-changer' or 'cunning'.

He'd be 'home-wrecker', no more than dirt,

while she was a hero or a harmless flirt.

His face would be judged in magazines,

Her policies and actions would steal the scenes.

She could walk alone at night

and not be blamed for any plight.

But he'd be whistled at in the street

or (wo)man-handled like a piece of meat.

And if his reputation were in any doubt,

his attacker would have an instant out.

There'd be 'no slots' for him at comedy night

though she could expect her name in lights.

He'd face the 'imaginary' glass ceiling

while she could succeed it whatever's appealing.

He'd have to struggle for every right

and she'd just claim he was too 'uptight'.

We wouldn't accept this for our men,

nor should we for women, ever again.

T.J. Collins

This Is Not Sex

A teacher drunk on a staff night out,

Too far gone to say no, no doubt.

This is not sex.

A married woman lies in her bed,

Husband thrusting into her, despite what she said.

This is not sex.

A campaigner for women's rights online,

Told she needs to be shown "a good time".

This is not sex.

A teenager under the age of consent,

An adult who acts on the "feelings" present.

This is not sex.

A student in town, in skirt and high heel,

Cornered by a friend who wants a quick feel.

This is not sex.

A journalist who changed her mind,

But her boyfriend, regardless, continues to grind.

This is not sex.

An accountant who wakes up in early December,

in a man's bed – how she got there, she just can't remember.

This is not sex.

A woman, any woman, who doesn't say yes,

Who isn't enthusiastic, who gives any less…

This is not sex.

T.J. Collins

Battlefield

Ten years later,
the war rages on,
ripping lives apart
piece by piece.

Casualties continue to fall,
not bodies but death
of friendships, relationships...
all that was and could be.

Flashbacks consume
at the slightest trigger,
still reliving the moment,
still anything but still.

The battlefield lies in ruins,
haunted by her violent past,
waiting for healing and renewal,
rebuilding her life
peace by piece.

T.J Collins

Shared Truths

She sits across the table

Speaking softly, avoiding my gaze.

The web begins to surround us,

A myriad of emotions surround us,

As she speaks of the violence that haunts her these days.

A taboo that is always unspoken,

Binds us tightly as it sets us free,

Causing confusion within us –

Relief and pure rage crash within us.

We can't escape the emotional debris.

But in our past, we are united,

A web of powerful bond.

We stand together against them,

Protect each other against them,

And look to the future beyond.

In her tale, I find hope –

The beauty of our delicate web.

There is no pity between us,

Just sisterhood and clarity between us,

As the power of taboo starts to ebb.

T.J. Collins

Rape

Rape

One word.

The word.

No-one speaks its name.

Rape.

Rips through her life like a hurricane,

No pattern but destruction,

Leaving silence.

Her silence.

Rape.

Everyone knows why.

They think they know why.

They believe it all.

Myths.

Lies.

Rape.

You sit there disgusted,

Disgusted at the word,

Disgusted at her.

She sits disgusted at herself

and I sit disgusted by you.

Who sits disgusted by him?

Rape.

One word.

The word.

We must speak its name.

T.J. Collins

Office Bitch

She sits at her desk, without a smile;
grim determination upon her face.
A glare strikes fear into others
and conversation is met with apparent disdain.

She sits at her desk while, not far away,
comments are made on her brusque demeanour.
The silent punch-line to a million jokes;
a pantomime villain for the modern world.

She sits at her desk – to her colleagues' relief –
If she appears, they scurry away
to safer ground or back to their work;
Any excuse to escape her 'vindictive' attacks.

She sits at her desk and no-one cares
about the person that lies within.
Her job is all that matters to them;
a self-fulfilling prophecy of a heartless machine.

She sits at her desk to hide from the world
and locks all her feelings inside.
One moment of weakness and the whole façade cracks;
everything she holds dear would break down.

She sits at her desk, unsure of herself,

not knowing how to relate.

Would they reject her if she let them in?

Would they just bend over and laugh?

She sits at her desk to escape the pain,

to escape the flashbacks and horrors of… that.

While she works, she can't see his face

or feel him inside her again.

She sits at her desk, without a smile;

grim determination upon her face.

A glare strikes fear into others

and conversation is met with apparent disdain.

T.J. Collins

Blame the Patriarchy
(for my mother)

If you will blame the man who molested me for my queer
sexuality
you might as well just blame the patriarchy.

Blame my father for the nights he didn't come home to you, and I
learned what love meant falling asleep next to your sweet
breath.

Blame your father for his strictness and harshness that he
passed on to you
in the form of a hard line on my spirit of dissent

Blame your second husband for his depression, and sex
addiction, that caused another marriage to collapse before my
eyes.

Blame the Catholic Church for covering up its scandals and
failing my tests of faith.

Blame the boys who touched my private parts in public, the ones
who spent my money freely while they told me that they loved
me, the ones who scared me, scarred me, raised their voices to
call me ugly names, took advantage if I ever shed my inhibitions,
made fun of me or refused to listen when I spoke my mind.

Blame the ones who left me lonely and the ones who never called back.

Blame the young man who raped me because I dared show up in his dorm room when invited.

Blame the men who fought me till I bit my tongue, who taught me with their words and actions that they could never love me like you did.

Blame them, and then tell me if it makes any difference

El Dia

Broken Petals

The stench of desperation lingering in the air, It forces itself in my face as I open the door to our house of cards. The distant memories of who I used to be are perfectly placed like trophies on your bookcase.

In the beginning it was you and I against the world but now the tears of broken petals run down and cut my face in the coldness of your every word.

Those words enveloped in barbed wire ripping at my pursuit of love, longing to be needed, but abandoned like an unwanted child snatched from its mothers womb.

Fractured pictures now represent what used to be our love, your lust, your pursuit of control. Without resistance you thrust your dominance upon me as I lay invisible and unmoved by your touch.

The cries of help silenced by the shadows of fear, and my lips padlocked by your insecurity.

You tell me I can't leave, what would become of a man like you, my mind screams run although my feet never gets the message.

Your persuasion suffocates my need to break free; no one can love me like you do those repetitive words play like a shattered record.

We are the silhouette of two bodies merely existing and we stand still as love has left us behind.

Starved of affection, my body has become your road map of abuse.

You tell me I can leave with one hand around my neck and my attempts become futile as your grip gets tighter.

Surrounded by a sea of self denial, the waves continue to wash over me every night as I watch you sleep. Your delicate breaths soft like the wind coming and going, while I remain drowning in unwept tears.

The one I knew and what I thought I loved is dead. A mask for the green eyed monster that was truly inside.

Shut away from the one's who were supposed to be the closest to me, alienated and wondering in oblivion, the darkness engulfs me and is now my closest friend.

Out of sight, out of mind.

The pain I have become an expert in pushing away and swallowing down has made me immune to the wounds, the blows and the bruises.

In my final shout, as you lay in a pool of blood and your mistakes, your excuses and your rage, I stand frozen over your lifeless body as death has done us apart.

Oge Ejizu

Genie

(A limerick for children whose imaginations are their only lifeline)

There was once a girl with spectacles that she did not need to see.

Instead she wore them at night for their marvellous memory erasing quality;

gone were his uninvited touches invading her bed,

erased were the 'you must be mistaken's that people she told said.

When wearing these glasses a little girl who believed in magic she could once again be.

Acia Eve

Untitled

Don't forget who you are

Don't lose what you know

You're not a possession, a plaything, a tool

You're fabulous specimen of humankind

There's a voice in your head

So keep speaking your mind

Remember your views, they're yours for the keeping

Don't put up, don't shut up

There's no place for submission

Build deeper foundations

Where your name is waiting

Be careful of sorrys

They're not always true

But above all else

Please don't forget you.

@extreme_crochet

I am the Phoenix

I am the Phoenix

I am the eternal fire

With my flame red hair

And my caustic tongue

I will rise again

Over and over

And come back every time stronger

Burning a path before me

I'll leave nothing but ashes

As I'm all out of goodness

So I offer no sanctuary

For I am the goddess

And you, you

You are nothing

@extreme_crochet

Fuck off

You know nothing of me

You know nothing of me

I would have waited for you

Would have crushed all your foes

But you made me a fool

Brought me down like a tree

I was graceful and willing

I was up for the taking

You know nothing of me

You know nothing of me

To treat me this way

Like I'm unworthy of you

Well, you know what to do

You can go screw yourself

And fuck off with your words

They mean nothing to me

You know nothing of me

You know nothing of me

So just stay away now

I do not want to know

How my beauty is great and my passionate soul

Don't you think I don't know

You can fuck off with that

@extreme_crochet

ID

Can I let my life be defined by you not him

Be a victim of grief not violence

Have comfort in the happiness of shared times

Like when we sparked like a green wood fire

All you damaged was my heart

He took away my soul

And now I am as empty as your are dead

@extreme_crochet

Untitled

My life, a constant crashing wave

Like some endless nightmare

Yet I'm awake

There are teasers of joy

Hints of amazement and

I'm smiling again

It's so nice to smile

Then I hear the loud boom

Of water on rock

That was the sound

Of my happiness shattered

Crushed again wand again

Like some hopeless crew

Of a doomed fishing vessel

Getting forever slammed

Into cliffs built for protection

What use are they against

The storm that my mind brews

I will be broken down

Smaller and smaller

Until only atoms are left

And emotions are useless

But the process is slow

And it causes me pain

So what shall I do

Too exhausted to swim

Too bruised to hold on

All I can do is give in

And give up my soul

@extreme_crochet

Untitled

I don't have a thigh gap

My legs join at the top

I've no idea if my mons

Is fashionable or not.

My breast are too small

To fit into a bra

My stomach has bloated

To the size of a car

There's lines on my face

But worse there is hair

It seems to want to grow everywhere

No creams, cleansers or lotions

Applied to my skin can stop it

From giving up and caving in

I have to accept that it

Comes to us all

Not all Cinderellas can go to the ball

The airbrush they use may as well be a gun

Pointing at women and saying

'Hey! You look wrong'

So maybe it's time we said

'Fuck you' to that crap

I'll grow old in my own way

So go swivel on that.   @extreme_crochet

120

Bloodlust

There you lay oozing
Blood ran cold, blood ran dry.
A solitary fly buzzing
Stunned by the echo of your death-cries
Stifled by your blood-constricted throat
Brutalised by a knife's gyration.

Sister, all your imagined wrongs
That moved his hirsute wrist
Insinuatingly through dark alleyways
Twitching inside an overcoat
Seeking your final submission
Calling out your guts.

Children peeking, unbelieving
Your mother and I are talking,
He says - blood-spilling
What kind of talking is that?
Let it be the last.

You will not be consigned to dust
Time must not heal
Nor memory conceal

Your blood will not congeal
Our actions.

This is not one more obituary
Not one more nail
Sealing the covers of our oppression
This is the lifting of the lid
To find the wellspring of our liberation

Come we will show men what fear is
When courage stalks a woman's raised fist.

Rahila Gupta

Passenger action

Tut-tutting
Cluck-clucking
Watch watching
Slowing down
Losing minutes
Missed the opening
Kept a lover waiting
The hairdresser, the boss, the doctor.

Down the line someone
Was under a train
Passive, tense no more
Making a statement.
My heart pumping
My stomach churning.
It could not be her
I left her
At home, under a sheet,
Sleeping
A short sleep
I hope.

This poem was written to commemorate the death of Balwant Kaur, an Asian woman who was brutally stabbed to death in the 80s by her husband in front of her children at the refuge to which she had escaped. The Balwant Kaur campaign held a fund-raising memorial at which this poem was first read.

Rahila Gupta

Roses from her Valentine

She waited, breath bated, for the gloom
To be dissipated by the heady scent of roses
Unfolding in the room.
Hoping, if they were sent
They'd arrive, neither drooping nor unscented.
So much has Valentine's Day wormed its way
Into hearts and purses in the West.

The rose - that is not worm-eaten - is fumigated
By a woman far away who grows it
Choked by the spray, breath abated,
Stirring life into dead earth.
The land is blooming but it grows no food
Never mind! The line of credit is extended,
Food floods in from the West.

That land is irrigated by water that cannot be spared.
Her child's thirst remains unmitigated.
She counts her pennies
While the fruit of her labour is transported
To loveless rooms - D.O.A. drooping on arrival.
So much has Valentine's Day wormed its way
Into hearts and purses in the West.

She too untimely drops her unscented head,

The rose perfecting spray works in its mysterious way.

Lovers, do not be incensed by roses unsent.

Many lives could be unknotted

If other tokens can be located.

Let Valentine's Day go uncelebrated

When you find out how its red roses originated.

Rahila Gupta

Emotional Gymnast

Your distance draws me close
like I can lessen it by choosing
just the right thing
at just the right time
seeking and grasping
for a fucking perfect place
where I'm just the right amount of happy
and you're just the right amount of sorry

Your passion is predicate
as you subconsciously premeditate
how you'll storm out later
so relief will swallow rage on your return
I want you to know
it's never without discomfort
my wounded hero
who never turns his back to me
and bows low when I leave the room

It's sick though
your love is purpose-shaped
snug with my desire for strangulation

Our pieces are no normal shape

but like a jigsaw, sometimes we make

a complete picture, squared off corners and all

Lynsey Hansford

The First Step

We are awake

Our justice lust

can't be sated

Our socialisation

is a mere complication

in rejecting oppression

Take a deep breath

and your sisters hand

and say "No...

...fuck your control

And what you think we should do

We are all women...

...and we don't answer to you"

Lynsey Hansford

My Place

I'm put in my place

a well worn and pleasant

lady-shaped space

The past smoothed the silhouette

and it's edges hold me tight

and provide just enough food

to feed me

and just enough comfort

to keep me

The girl next door

used to stick her hand out

So they cut it off

and told us in syrupy voices

that we weren't like her

We were one of them

Our honeycomb home

is enough for us

I am helping to carve out

a slot for my daughter

Never have they looked smaller

or less inviting   Lynsey Hansford

130

Room 101

Plucking every single hair from my pubic region with agonising care, douching with chemical solutions until my stinging vagina smells like a newly cleaned bathroom and feels like a dry mouth.

Words fill my closed mouth and bottle neck behind my plump, red lips on the day they come for my daughter but now it's too late.

Lynsey Hansford

The Lie

And the lie was born
in seductive persuasion
and lived to destroy.

But what is a lie?

It is a reality
a possible truth.

Our life was like that lie

Smiling, happy, compliant.
Lies becoming truths.

And a long-life-fear
of twisted realities
has been hard to live.

So, now you are dead
and I have survived it all.

I am not that child
born into that lie
smiling, happy, well-behaved,

crying and fearful.

It all died with you.
It is buried, it is gone
I walked the fire
and burned you from my soul

Barbara Hughes

Growing Up

Born a Baby Boomer

in an only used on Sundays front roomer baby

but rumour has it I made a dramatic entrance

as I was forceped into that front room

and our symbiotic discordant screams

ricocheted round heavy curtains and dark furniture

But I was made a good girl

a well-behaved with knees nagged together when I sat sort of

girl

didn't speak till spoken to polite girl

seen and not heard quiet girl

sweet smiling guarded part of the wallpaper girl

abused and beaten afraid of life and shadows girl

ready to break loose growing girl..........ready steady ......

Barbara Hughes

Girl and Woman

I am a woman

I am sixty three years old

I have three children and nine grandchildren

now I havI am a girl

I am eleven years old

soon I will sit my Eleven Plus examination

and I will go to Grammar School

to not go to Grammar School

would be 'unthinkable' says my Father

My Mother is beautiful

I have a handsome Father

so he says.

I have two brothers

they are both younger than me

and I love them both

only one brother and I love him

I have good friends

I have a job a house and a car

I enjoy most of my life

sometimes I go a bit crazy

then I take pills

this has been happening on and off

most of my life

I have friends who understand me

I have children who don't

This is not their fault

This is my fault

But it is His fault in the first place

If I try to imagine a different girl who is eleven

If I try to imagine a different life

then I can't imagine a different sixty three year old woman

I have no idea what she would be like

at least I know who I am

this sixty three year old woman

I know her crazy as she is

I am glad I have the children I have

I am glad I have the friends I have

But the life I have is difficult to live

Barbara Hughes

No Escape

I wish you two would stop fighting
Ma head's been thumpin' all day.
If you'd just give me peace for a minute   or two
go and watch tele or find something to do
but just get out of ma way.

He's no come in from the pub yet
an' ma clubman's due the night
I could take it oot the electric tin
I could go and see what pub he's in
but that would just start a fight.

I canny see how we're tae manage
he got paid off the end o' last week
since then he's been comin' in drunk every night
he's spent a' the money it just isnae right
but it's more than ma life's worth tae speak.

He's one that can't cope wi' his problems
well he's no had much o' a life
his maw died at thirty his dad used tae drink
he canny feel love, well that's what I think
but it's a hard job bein' his wife.

An' I listen tae some of these women
shouting out about what we should do
An' I know in my heart that they're right and I'm wrong
for I canny believe this is where I belong
for I've got my life tae live too.

But this is my bed and I'll lie here
I took him for better or worse
anyway wi' four weans I've nowhere to go
I'm no from round here, so there's no-one I know
an' I just couldn't bear a' the fuss.

So I wish you two would stop fightin'
It just seems to go on and on
and he'll come through that door full o' sorries an' beer
and sad explanations I don't want to hear
an' that's another day gone.

But maybe one day I will leave him
And I'll pack up the weans and we'll run
An' I'll never look back and I'll never regret
There'll be no more fear nor pain nor debt
An' I'll lift up my face to the sun.

Barbara Hughes

I Can Cry Now

I can cry for you now little girl.

I can weep tears and my tears will pour

out of me as I cry for you.

I will find all the pieces,

those fragments that flew up and out

in a thousand directions

still attached.

Long fragile threads, knotted and twisted.

Hidden fragments, broken pieces.

I will find them all and I will tie them

together gently.

And I will say, look at this,

look at the woman you will become.

So I will cry for you now.

I will cry for the lost hours in the night,

and in the day

and in all those years.

Lost hours, lost life.

I will cry for the pain

and I will cry for the fear.

I will cry when I remember.

But I will say this

look at the woman you have become.

Fighting Cliché Spirit

I've put my shoulder to the wheel

I've put my back into it

shoved my best foot forward

I've thrown my chest out

and snapped my shoulders back

- hoping one of them wouldn't clash with   the wheel -

kept on my toes

and put my ear to the ground

- difficult with chest out shoulders back etcetera but I

persevered -

my nose was always to the grindstone

I've kept an eye out

and stayed alert

my fingers are in many pies

and I'm always ready to lend a hand

my lip is zipped because Mum's the word

I've joined in ganged up

stood my ground dug my heels in

put money in the tin and a cheque in the post

my eye was always on the ball

and I grasped it with both hands

I've embraced challenged

never conceded defeat

never turned my back

always elbowed my way in

been on my knees

ground my teeth

put a smile on my face

cheered up because I always believed it would never happen

always had time for a cup of tea

my heart has always been in it

and has sometimes forgiven

but I have also blamed and lashed out

and at the end of the day

what does life have in store

well The Patriarchy is still there

and white people still don't get it

so what do I do

I pick myself up dust myself down and

start all over again

because I'm a woman and I'm still here

So I'll sing you a song

it's the song of a woman who's trying to be strong

Barbara Hughes

31st December, 2012

1.

A new conditioner
high heels, a too tight skirt
party party
sometimes outside in snow
forbidden smoke
icy sky
clinking of glasses, a jump
into new year
no clock ticks, dancing
a familiar smell,
Abba under the Christmas tree
sips of water before bed
brushed teeth
sleeping bag,
lying in dreams

> socks on carpet, shoe size 11
> who's there, what's he doing,
> hands, too big, under my –
>> am I dreaming, is this
>> a dream, is this

a nightmare –

2.   –

                     --

3.

tele- tele
telephone

waiting.

for a silver car
withblue lights.

Katharina Maria Kalinowski

3rd January, 2013

Tiredness
Leaking
through my body

rusted tears

boiling water
trickling into a coffee filter

            drip

                drip

                    drip

                lavender eye circles
                matching my new jumper

                pyjama
                in a rubbish bag

                DNA
                on cotton buds

my coffee

will be cold

when I come home   Katharina Maria Kalinowski

January. February. March.

I stop counting.
The window is open

the moonlight
tastes of bitter chocolate

my body
has forgotten how to sleep.

I lie and hear
how it's getting brighter outside.

Minutes
breathe under my skin

the moths
are switching their lights off.

I've stopped counting.

Katharina Maria Kalinowski

Mother Blame

You would have noticed

Yeah, you, I'm talking to all of you

You were sure to notice something:

There's the foundation of this absurd conceit!

The Old Masters: they well understood*

How our gaze is never there

Not at the moment of deceit

All points on the canvas draw away from such acts

The painting's gaze is peeling potatoes

We're washing dishes, watching our TVs

While the abuser's plan unfolds off corner

We cannot know all that is behind the curtain

About the mechanisms of the human mind

How we notice its workings only after the fact

When it is too late for reason to react

When hindsight tells us that thin ice might crack

But we cannot change the plot we did not plan

Only accept its lessons, share its warnings

Accept the challenges of our family's fate

Accept because we knew too late

But you seem so sure of your authority on this

You would have noticed all of that?

All the 'goings on' as you so call them

The behind closed doors, the matter of fact

How wounding are your words to me!

How startling your conceit

Would you have noticed the shoe of Icarus too?

As it brushed against your cheek?

Musee des Beaux Arts – W.H.Auden

Clare Lavery

Anonymous

There is no knowing when it will end

This need for anonymity

We sometimes tire, grow weary of

The shadow plays; evasions

To avert the prying eyes

The curiosity hunters

Appeased with little white family lies

Each one reminds me of the shame

The setting apart

From a life with open doors

And an ever trusting heart

No skeletons in their cupboards

No case notes or family court orders to stash away

No fear of community search lights

Hunting down that corner of obscurity

The holes in our new family narrative

Exposing the suffering

He dumped on us

There is no knowing

When we will ever see their type of normality again

Be ourselves joyfully, unashamedly

The cover story cloak abandoned

A shield to their prejudice

Protection from their malicious expectations

Anonymous

Clare Lavery

Failure to protect

The media is full of preying Jimmys

Yours preyed from within

Tampering with the floor plans

From early on in your relationship

He dismantled

Deactivated maternal alarm systems

Managed the impressions

Of the outsiders

Looking in

With all your judgements pre-empted

Reason short-circuited

To suit him

He damaged the foundations of your kin

Disrupting the communication lines between you

Creating an illusion of a safe home

To hide in

His rules of engagement were cloaked

His intention skilfully disguised

Safely operating in your embrace

All obscured to the untrained eye

He was protected by your trust

From the outside

He was undetectable
Rather polished when looking in.

But when his game was up
He was caught right in the act
Someone had to be responsible
You had only thought to trust
So the outsiders came in
And held you to account
With difficult questions
With their insinuations and assumptions
Held you equally responsible
For all that was in doubt

Hindsight can be used to judge you
And your propensity to trust
Someone must be held accountable
For the predators in our midst
How would society investigate
Those undetected Jimmys?
The ones we call our Father
Our favourite Uncle, our next of Kin
The ones who single-handedly
Destroyed our sense of trust
So you tolerate their insults

You take it on the chin

The answer to their questions

Must surely lie within?

Clare Lavery

Unspoken

You pass the vintage sugar bowl

My unspoken words sit politely

I have to silence a lot of me, you see

I offer my storylines gingerly at your table

My hushed up hidden life concealed

Face down on your *Cath Kidson* cloth

I dare not turn over a single fact

That is a rather risky reveal for me

The truth is stranger than reality, you see

My front door key unlocks

No neat forgiving plots

Uncomfortable storylines explode there

Uncertainty replaces domestic bliss

The unexpected and unseen unfold

My collusion in our *Country Living* friendship

Will depend on some conversational *hide and seek*

Your taboos invite me to employ creativity with all this

It's your respectable polish that's the problem

It glues my truth face down

'Delighted to welcome me again'

'Good for friends to come round'

Skeletons in cupboards and home baked cupcakes

Would make such an unlikely match

Telling you I am a domestic violence victim

Mentioning my journey, its twists, its turns

Would not fit into our chat

Better to airbrush my feelings

Push my awkward crumbs from your table

Enquire about your life and loves

Choose the path of least revealing

Tell you a digestible and appetising fable

Expose rather a lot less of me

More's the pity you see

For fear that your lack of compassion

Might spoil our nice cup of tea

Clare Lavery

Digitally removed

Wedding finery with matching ties

Sunday best smiles

The photographer fixes us

 Lined up as kin

Groom right

Bride to the left

His face is immortalised

Glued in back row right

He's standing just in front of the velvet drape

Dressed up in an artificial grin

The Husband

The Father

The Uncle

A Child abuser within

His hand rests on my son's shoulder

The most difficult part to remove

In its place now hangs another curtain

Digital magic done

No trace of that face in the collection

Contours airbrushed with trickery

New technology battles memory

But memory has certainly won

Remember how good he was

At posing for the family album?

Creating passports of normality

 Captured on every occasion

Years spent in silent regret

Trying to avoid the recollection

His harmful presence left

He's still haunting our future celebrations

The hint of him hanging

Obscured by a collective curtain

Impervious to our survivor determination

He's the poltergeist behind the set on every occasion

The spirit blowing out the birthday candles

His exit so badly stage managed

Forever Just off camera

He's the shadow of a negative within

The gate crasher in the narrative

Eternally loitering there

An echo in all our childhood snaps

Can you see him, still smiling, behind that chair?

Clare Lavery

Definitions of harm

Harm

It's a long way down

Freefall without the parachute

With no guarantee of safe landings

Life rushing past in descent

It's the unexpected force

The heart-crush on impact

The rearrangement of windows in all your walls

The changing of all familiar measurements

The rubbing out of our past family maps

The brutal and terrifying fall

Nothing to guide us at all

The humiliation of a well intentioned mother

Harm

It's all the assumptions of blame

The din of the professionals

Their unspoken assumptions

Their endless patronising questions

About my role in his game

The perceived responsibility as a mother

The gossip in the community about you

The questions about your role as his lover

It's the real 'me' that got lost in this relentless process

It's that sudden label of the 'other'

It's the humiliating of the non-offending mother

Harm

It's finding resilience to survive the unpredicted

To put one foot in front of another

It's the sticking of shards from the family frame

With messy glue of any love left in your kitchen cupboards

Doing this all alone without him forever

It's a kaleidoscope, it's ever-changing,

It's perpetually in motion

This churning of conflicting emotions

The love you had, its sudden loss,

The agony of his unspeakable acts

Trying desperately to shape

A new, plausibly coherent path

It's the stumbling, the setbacks, the growing stigma

The guilty by association to an offender

As the non-offending mother

Harm

It's the memory of all those family plans and hopes

Shattered in one split second of knowing

The fragrance of a family life in first bloom

Distilled in murmurs of past moments together

The sweet taste of our once peaceful days

With the detritus of family life all around us

Our innocent toddlers at play

All that of their promise we shared

All shattered by his own calculation

In one inconceivable moment of power

It's this which stays with us forever

With the silencing of trust in one another

It's his harm lingering all around us

It's his offending forever

It's the being forced by circumstances beyond us

Into starting anew as another

So, don't call me a non-offending mother

Clare Lavery

For A Woman Somewhere

For a woman somewhere,

yesterday was no ordinary day.

She woke up with her body as hers,

But now her woman is violated

After he forced himself to dwell In her temple.

The night no longer dances in her world,

the sky runs for cover,

the moon fears that

if it ends its nights shift too early

no one would find her body

if she decides to let it die with the pain.

If only sound travelled faster than wickedness,

maybe someone would have heard her screams that day.

There are some men who love to swallow women into

nothing but legs to pull with force. They are simply cowards

with hands. Their teeth's are always looking for bodies to sink

into.

If you look closely you will see the bite marks on their own

bodies.

Everyday a new woman is muted into years of silence.

But she will not go down without a fight

Her voice will scream for the million other women
who have seen faces familiar to yours.

She will be your nightmares,
Her screams will deafen you into an apologetic existence.
You will regret ever thinking rape
was a game of legs versus power.

Some nights she is crying on the bathroom floor
Some days she is telling the world her pain
with the word 'survivor' tattooed between her legs.
Her body is still trying to decide between strength or broken

Your daughters face is too familiar,
you wonder why she looks so much like you
at the time you were raped.
You wonder if monsters will find her too,
if her body is beautiful enough and might ask for it
If her smile is too bright and might get the attention of ugly souls

You do not want to tell her
That the monsters she thought existed as a child
...grew up as well
and now walk on the street disguised as rapists,

And screams do not scare him.
He loves the sound of women disappearing into helplessness.

Your daughter is sitting on the couch as you stare at her,
You wish you prepared her for the war while she was in your
womb,
You wonder if she knows that
you once fought for her non-existence at the back of a van.
If she knows you think she is so beautiful
it hurts you to tell her that for a woman somewhere
yesterday was no ordinary day.

This same mouth also reminds her
That love is beautiful,
And someone will carry her heart in their palms
like it is a rare breed,
I wonder if she will ever question why your view on love
is a string of contradictions.
Some nights you are crying on the bathroom floor
Some days you are telling the world your pain
With the word 'survivor' tattooed between your legs.
Her body is still trying to decide between strength or broken

                                        Theresa Lola

Anna in the Ashes

Anna's in the ashes,

Mad as leaves.

Harvests her tears

And watches him

Grind them

For his bread

"You're mad" he said.

And true enough

The look in her eyes

Is wild and hunted,

Her baby cries,

Her hair's a mess,

Her arse is fat,

She smokes too much,

And shakes and sighs,

"It's too much" he says

"To live with that".

Poor old farmer

To live with that.

Leaves crack against the window,

And he rattles out the charges,

"You left the fire unlit,
and didn't clear the ashes".

So with ash in her hair,
She forgives his trespasses,
But wanders on his dreams,
Like a hungry fox,
Leaving many snowy footprints.

The empty fields
Trail away to nothing,
And more snow on the way
Will cover any trace,
Where she's running to keep up
With the songs of her babies
And the knock of her heart,
And the knowledgeable wind,
That rips her face.

The snow turns to sleet,
And the mark of her feet
Comes round in a circle
To the same old place,

Where he waits,

With his shotgun.

So is it better to be mad or dead?

Runs with her babies

Out into the night,

"You'll die" he said

"Of cold, and raving snowstorms".

But her eyes and the night

Are hard and bright.

Jan Martin

Invisible Until

I heard of magic you can do

When the house goes dark with fear

Where if you keep stock-whisper-still,

You stay invisible until It's safe to reappear

So under crushing otherness

You vanish like a prayer,

You hold your breath, and barely grow,

Til you're the only one to know

There's anybody there.

Jan Martin

Another Perspective on Sex

I'm ashamed of my sex life.

I'm ashamed that I'm 23 years old & still have no idea what sex feels like.
I know the mechanics: panties, boxers, pulled down, if not completely off, erect penis penetrates wet vaginal canal.

He begins heaving heavy breaths as I turn away.

Eyes stay closed until he makes an "O" face, until he stops moaning, until he convinces himself he's satisfied me & I comply silently as he rolls of me to compose himself for the next go-round.
But there has never been a next round ringing roses of sweet sensuality.

The only marathons we run is he away from me, eyes staring straight through as he walks right past me. I've never existed within or beyond bedsheets.
Or his moving my drum back to its proper place at the top of my bookcase.
A coy smile jokingly says to me, "It's like I was never here."
I respond but he tells me, "Don't make that face."

Hiding my feelings is nearly impossible, just as impossible as it is to not want to remove the scars carved into my pussy, signed, "Good times found here." "Fear not the need for commitment." "This is a one time deal."

I've been the training session for marathons between thighs that look nothing like this pair that touch too often, that weigh too much, evoking thoughts,
"At least you don't have to think about them when you spread them apart."
I feel marked by inadequacy, only able to satisfy when less than or equal to satisfactory.

I've learn how to pleasure myself by reminiscing about my mediocrity of just getting a man's attention, of just getting a man's hand to pat my ass because that's the softest act of intimacy I've known.
I worry the last time I had sex will be the last time I have sex.

Some say don't hold your breath, but if you've survived inhaling outside toxins, you'd realize I'd rather hold tight to my own carbon dioxide if I have to experience asphyxiation.

I regret that I've never let someone in on my own terms. I yearn companionship when I'm most alone.

Demolished boundaries rebuilt by semi-anonymous architects.

They detect something is wrong with the foundation, but by the time the levees break, I find they were able to escape to another state of being free within arms I thought would be mine.

But they heeded the warning signs, left early enough before the storm said it was too late, but this body never made it.

Death's misery was always too enticing.

I've relied on finding comfort in the worst form of intimacy: good.

Good enough to distract me, good enough to wrap me in the warmth of lust's self-deception, going nowhere form under covers, amongst the nights stars sprinkling twilight dust upon my blasphemous acts compromising darkness' integrity.

So I repent mercilessly, scream muted prayers on the grounds behind my eyelids,

"Lord I'm being laid down to sleep. Make me a soul, on that I can keep because

I'm dying trying not to stay awake as I pray my insecurities be taken away" through technical bull rides.

I've paid the price with shame tokens for rides without actually riding, finding time only when it was bad timing.

I have to remind myself constantly history doesn't always have to repeat itself, that there will be a next time, that there's more in store than chance encounters to knock boots for added notches on bed posts elevating egos who aren't utilizing their full potential.

I just want to be able to look into their eyes.

I just want to be able to feel every part of their being inside of me because I'd like to believe that's what sex actually feels like without technicalities, when it's not just a mechanical production, which is why I'm ashamed of my sex life. I'm 23 years old & I've had sex but as of yet have no idea what sex feels like & sometimes I'm not sure if I'll learn that lesson.

Victoria M Massey

Flame

Today I realised I'm tougher than I thought

You tried to keep me down and break me

And weak as I was I fought

In little ways I held my own

Tiny rebellions, your power I erode

Caught in your abuse and anger

I put myself together

And from the ashes I arose

My flame was brighter than I ever knew

Even amidst all you did, still it grew

I'm tougher than I thought

I'm stronger than I knew

My flame burns brighter now

Because of the abuse from you

Claire Meadows-Haworth

Haunting

I'm living with a ghost

Haunting inside my head

It's wails drown out my thoughts

Even though it's dead

I'm living with a ghost

Haunting all my dreams I buried it some time ago

And yet still hear its screams

I'm living with a ghost

Haunting all my memories

Locked behind my doors

It always finds the keys

I'm living with a ghost

Haunting all of me

I'm bringing in the Exorcist

And then I can finally be free.

Claire Meadows-Haworth

PHOTOGRAPHS

Misty-silence, early- morning, curtains twitching, soft, blue light

Whispered-voices, T.V's switching, some heard shouting, in the
night

"Such a nice man"

"Who'd have thought?"

"Devoted-couple"

"Life goes on"

"Was she leaving?"

"Seeing someone?"

Rumour runs his marathon...

In the dawn, two bodies lying, in the circus-ring of police

Speculating, picking up, our pictures from the mantelpiece...

We two smiling, drinking cocktails

Calm, blue sea and beach, behind

My smile speaks early love and romance

Lying, gentle, on my mind...

Another picture - leaves are turning
In the autumn-afternoon
Smiles are fading, I am learning
Winter-storms are coming soon...

Final picture - Christmas-morning
Over, by the Christmas-tree
His body-language speaks no warning
Or the way he looks at me -
Night must fall and find me crying
How I dread this time of year
New Year's Day will find me lying
In this three-ring-circus, here...
Prints and photographs are taken
Bodies shifted, crime-scene sealed
Neighbourhood is grey and shaken
'Murder-Suicide' revealed...

People reeling, from the danger
No need to lock your front-doors, tight
He was my partner! Not a stranger!
No-one's coming in the night!..

No-one's creeping-up, to hurt you
The killer's gone - the Murderer is dead!
He was the man I gave my life to
Who said he loved me - shared my bed...
Yes, the man who said he loved me
Loved me to eternity
The man who ranted, pushed and shoved me
With so much 'love'.. he murdered me!

My photo, in the paper, smiling
A headline read - a page is turned
Another crime-statistic filing
A 'tragedy' - with 'lessons- learned'

Woman rising, in the morning
Reads and listens, to the news
Tries to search his face, for warning
Tries to read his eyes, for clues

What he thinks, he isn't saying
She's praying the bad atmosphere will cease
And all the while, her eyes are straying
To photos... on a mantelpiece.....

Claire Moore

SHUT UP

They said shut up

When I spoke of sexual attacks since the age of 6.

They said shut up

When I asked my father to stop beating me.

They said shut up

When I asked why my mother needed to be broken to give birth

They said shut up when I asked for higher mathematics.

They said shut up when I asked for a boy's education.

They said shut up

When I was pregnant and unmarried.

They said shut up

When I asked why I only got half the pay-cheques of men in my office.

They said shut up

When those men molested me.

They said shut up

When I heard men speak of abuse as if it was nothing.

They said shut up at length today

For speaking out about violence within my own family.

I no longer shut up.

And for that

I have been shunned.

By all of them.

At seventy one.

Mary Moylan

Who am I to say "no"?

I say "no", but you do not hear me.

My soul cries out "no", but you do not hear me.

My tears stream down, but you do not see them.

My body is shrinking, but you do not see this.

My spirit is being crushed, but you do not notice.

The lady in the red kameez scolds:

"If not marrying now, when?"

The bearded man with the paan shrills:

"*besharam*, what about your dad's *izzat*?"

Their *izzat*, their honour, their status, their community.

Who am I to demand, to desire, to dream?

Who am I to think, to create, to break?

Who am I to lie naked, to arch my back?

Who am I to breathe, to live?

Who am I?

Who am I?

This day is not my own:

This dress, these jewels, these clinking bangles are not mine.

This man pressing against me: you are not for me.

These people greedily munching, not seeing or hearing.

"Husband", "daughter", "mother", "father" –

These words mean nothing, I mean nothing.

I am nothing.

I cannot breathe, I cannot be.

I will die if I stay, I will be crushed.

I must save me, I must save my spirit. I must live.

I must run, I must fight, I must love, I must feel.

I must, I must.

I am alone, but I am me.

I have nightmares, but I am me.

I have no family, but I am me.

I break fast alone, but I am me.

I have me.

I am me.

Huma Munshi

What's that?

What's that?

I heard you say, why are you wearing that dress that way?

Skirt it too low, top too tight.

Change it,

Don't make me raise my hand before you put this right.

Your mine and that's how you will stay,

a bird in my cage locked up tight,

never really being allowed to have the freedom to feel flight.

Your eye shadow is too dark,

lipstick too bright,

wipe it off quick before you start a fight.

Trapped in the dark in the depths of my cage,

will I ever have the strength to break free?

Deep in the dark of the night sky a bird flies free,

one day that just might be me,

soaring high in the nights sky out of the darkness and into the light!

Kelly Nesbitt

No Escape

Against the wall, she shields her face,
appalled by what will now take place.
She's been here many times before,
too scared to break out through the door
to her utopia: safe space.

He said he loved her charm, her grace
and, when they met, that was the case
but now it's power that he loves more
against the wall.

She scarcely sleeps because he'll chase
round nightmares where she has to race
away from hurt that's always raw.
The pain shoots to her very core
yet he takes care to leave no trace
against the wall.

Nicky Phillips

I Am More Than Melanin

You mould

and rearrange the beat of the drum that pounds through every

part of our melanin.

Our culture is not for sale yet still -

you whitewash the attributes that encapsulate our Queens.

Doing away with their natural authenticity,

parading your

bootleg versions in every barbershop,

every hair shop,

every magazine inscribed with your Afrocentric imitations.

Showcasing European women without the curvatures that shape

our Queens and straight noses

pointed directly into the culture you love to misrepresent.

I mean, who are we?

We are the ghetto stains that fill your clothes shops.

The angry black women that fill your TV production companies

minority quota.

We -

are not educated,

nor are we beautiful but reminders -

that we are Queens will only ever be your maids,

your cleaners,

your token friends.

The mothers and sisters of men who -

are criminalised by your media and who's blood -

paint far too many of our local streets red.

Your children's school dinner ladies and your men's erotic

fantasies.

Advertising shows that the most attractive features of a black

woman are her -

derriere and her hair. As long as kinks are loose and her

melanin isn't darker than the cocoa robbed from her native land.

Diluted for your tasting,

of course.

Our women raise erections not expectations in the playground of

your men's minds. And -

my, my, my can she can whine,

because that's all black girls do, right?

Your "jungle fever' an excuse for heavy petting and disprescting

her inner being.

Dehumanized with every thrust and throat hold,

it doesnt matter if she says no,

after all -

animals can't talk.

She can let the braids fall down her back in submission to her

master but never should she speak.

Never should her eloquence or education

be made the centre of conversation.

Let's stick to simple statements like,

"Your hair is kind of like a sponge can I touch it?"

Or,

"No, no, no it's more like carpet, can you brush it?"

Spoken only after you

and the hands of your ancestors invade the crown of our temples

in order to steal the self-worth and value you've tried so hard to

break.

You can no longer fake -

the intertwining of our histories by -

purchasing fake bums and gelling down your baby hairs or

re-introducing cainrows as high-fashion whilst continuing to

depicting our darker Queens as well,

quite simply

"less than classically beautiful,"

as Viola Davis once heard.

Your police officers wrote the book on "How To Get Away With

Murder".

No wonder they got shook when Shonda exposed their secrets

and their lies.

Don't despise these truths.

We are not ignorant fools.

You want our beauty without our culture,

without the pain found in our melanin,

without the stain left upon us by society.

Our strength has never fallen and whilst you choose

to depict our history with men who our

Queens have not birthed and -

take our Daishikis and African prints to make

menswear shirts and ZARA skirts.

Whilst you crown JLo, Malckemore, Iggy and Ed

as the Kings & Queens of Hip Hop, Rap, Soul and RnB instead -

of the black artists who inspired,

collaborated and in some cases

surpass them in talent and excellence,

we -

will continue to be more than what you choose to see.

I am Shoshana Johnson.

The invisible US Soldier who

whilst serving in the Iraq was single mother who became a

prisoner of that war.

I am April Ericsson-Jackson.

The invisible Areospace Engineer at NASA.

I am Deesha Dyer.

The White House's invisible Social Secratary.

I am Isabel Dos Santos.

The world's richest invisible black woman.

I am the Chief Surgeon at your hospital.

I am the Head Mistress at your child's private and

comprehensive school.

I am your police officer, your lead detective and your Judge.

I am your MP and your UN Representative.

I am MORE than melanin.

I am a WOMAN.

And I -

Am a Queen.

Stephanie Popoola

Rush Hour Hand

I love London but I HATE rush hour!

Packed into tunnels like mice in a maze,

it just gets too much.

Bodies forged together by the joint desire to get home.

Forgetting our social principles and walking in our primitive

states.

Elbows in stomachs,

armpits in faces

and yes -

bags on feet,

no-one here's a VIP.

Here at rush hour where -

smart shirts and battered briefcases go head to head with

dirtied converses and travellers ruck sacks.

In this place

we are all same except for -

the elderly,

the physically challenged

and the pregnant of course!

Those we respect and create room for.

Reminding ourselves of our social principles as our moral

systems are put on stage

for the eyes of the secret onlookers peering over their

newspapers,

pretending to be busied by their Kindles

or reading their 50 Shades of Grey.

Do you know how many people went missing during rush hour

in 2014?

Or that roughly over 3.5 million people commute during rush

hour each year?

Or that in the last decade there has been an increase of 74% in

tube suicides?

I bet you didn't know this?

I bet you didn't know that last year I joined an estimated

400,000 women who are sexually abused every year in broad

daylight.

That the hand of a man unknown to me found his way through

society.

Pushing and pressing himself past the school girls,

the business women,

the pregnant mothers,

the female students

and the female tourists.

He pushed and pressed himself past these women

till his had found the back of my thigh.

Till it snaked itself around the crease of my behind and waited a

while.

Stealing buckets of my innocence,

my value and my being.

Riding me of a face,

a name,

a heart and creating something cold from bitter shame.

Allow me to further explain,

as his unwelcomed hand groped my thigh and then my behind,

I felt naked.

My shame covered by the unconcerned bodies of others,

unaware and unconcerned with my fear.

I thought it was a bag,

never thought it'd be a hand,

never dreamed it'd be a man

tearing and shredding away at my safety and using me as he

pleased.

Silenced by my fear I froze,

turning to find outstretched the hand of a man

I did not permit to touch me.

His eyes ignited with perverted desire.

His darkened face cleared to reveal something I never expected.

I saw someone's father,

someone's brother,

someone's son

staring in my face filled with shock and embarrassment.

Me -

still frozen,

too afraid to move in fear that I would provoke another groping.

The train doors open

and a sea of people pour out of the carriage,

whilst another wave fills it.

Taking with them the rush hour hand,

the man who's hand was not permitted to touch me.

His face leaves my mind but his touch and his abuse is seared

into the flesh of my thigh

and has left the imprint of his eyes upon my behind.

I shook,

so hard that my teeth created earthquakes in the city of my

heart.

But just like him,

just like them

I'll disappear into the sea of bodies

that ride along the rush hour tide.

I love London

but I can't stand rush hour,

can you?

Stephanie Popoola

I Have A Secret

You were meant to catch my whispers.

Use the bones in your body to hold my every tear,

allowing the vibrations from my quaking heart to find refuge in

your marrow.

You were meant to keep me.

Your beard reminding me of the forestry in Narnia and this

alternate reality we visited far too often.

Instead I gather memories

of your once smoky laugh filling rooms and hearts.

Candy necklaces remind me of the oath we made that sealed my

fate.

At 9,

you became apart of my many secrets.

Secrets wrapped in bubblegum, Hello Kitty plasters and double-

sided sticky tape.

Tucked away in the soles of my tattered size 4 plimsoles and the

creases of my Spice Girls diary

are questions I never dared allow to escape my raspberry

flavoured lips.

Questions clumsily fused together with half truths and forgotten

bruises.

From 9 to 14 you ruined the best of part of me.

Exploring every torrid fantasy and completing yourself within my velvet cove.

"No-one else needs to know."

Your nightly mantra.

The opal moonlight exposing the midnight beauty of my stretch

marks and scars,

forever painting a trail of memories filled with unfathomable

lewdity and a yellow brick road transporting me

to what used to be NeverLand.

This rusty tin shed

that housed your devilish paradise and my unending hell.

At least now I know,

that angelic tones and pure smiles hide hot lies.

At least now I know,

that I was never really blind.

Your callous heart scratching at my skin through my intimates,

with splintered fingernails ripping the purity of my youth before

their walls were marked by nature's crimson Christening.

You became an unclean memory in the cracks of my heart.

You were meant to keep me.

But like odd socks I lose people,

somewhere between the laundry basket and the dryer I lose

people.

I lost Dr. Jekyll and gained your Mr. Hyde.

The devious monster you tried so hard to hide.

I have secrets

And so do you.

Stephanie Popoola

Things we think of to comfort our minds

When looking at history and reading of mothers'
Stories so tragic our hearts can't take in
Of children dying, leaving families with longing
In numbers so great their sadness wearing

How could they cope with a grief so relentless?
The burden was lessened as so many tasted
The pain that they felt at the loss which they suffered.
These are the things which comfort our minds.

When women we know share abuse they've encountered
Some think it isn't as bad as they say.
"He sounds a bit like a boyfriend I once knew,
Who argued and frittered our money away.

I left him; it's easy. I went to my parents.
They gave me the space and means to start new."
But what they're not seeing are wounds he's inflicted
And no one to turn to which also means you.

"You see that man there? The one in the jumper,
His brother rapes women," but what they all think...
This can't be the case; he seems rather pleasant
And jokes at the bar and buys all the drinks.

She must have said yes, and then changed her desire.
That poor man now has to live with the shame.
But, wait... he still works and became a Director
While she sits alone and cradles the blame.

'Coz this wouldn't happen to me and my loved ones.
These are the things to comfort our minds.

Mary Rugman

Fear breeding fear

This anxious tense annoying place
Pickled with trauma peppered with stress,
Not part of any divine plan
Nor my preference I confess.

A remnant, a recall, a moment
That fearful flutter inside,
Breath waiting for the next train
Pumped, poised, eyes wide.
Expectations alter slowly
Natures instinctive force,
Fear breeds fear now as we watch
Sad nature take her course.

Roweena Russell

In the shadow of some things

It becomes easy not to grow
When the sky seams to hide from you,
Even harder to love
When nobody really wants to.

Feeling alone is uncomplicated
The patterns rushing through like blood,
Feeling better must be easier than this
I would explore it if I really could.

In the shadow of some things
It becomes very easy to die,
There are no arrests or court room justice
Because nobody bothers to ask why.

When rain nor shine finds you
Nothing gets to you direct,
Trust gets diluted quickly
The entire world becomes suspect.

But, in the shadow of some things,
The soil holds its wealth for later,
So the moment the sun gets to it
Growth explodes and the life even greater.

Nothing gets to you direct,

Trust gets diluted quickly

The entire world becomes suspect.

But, in the shadow of some things,

The soil holds its wealth for later,

So the moment the sun gets to it

Growth explodes and the life even greater.

Roweena Russell

The tide is out

Last year, I sat and listened to the sea weed dry.

Understanding that I was getting old.

I knew my tears when I watched them cry

They were mine I knew it, I had been told.

A lot had passed since now and then.

Nights are not sleeping, babies are growing children are

weeping

Adults are knowing that nothing changes in the day light

The worst of things don't grow right

All sorts of things walk towards the plight

What did you for bring me into this night?

Roweena Russell

Words are wasted

Words are wasted when they are used as ammunition

Missiles in the brain reminding me what went wrong,

The notes in my head scratch my ears

With each chorus each verse and wound me with every old song.

I repeat it in my head just in case for a moment

Every word said was not pounding me,

Forgetting at times that feelings go dormant

Say it once its costly, but utter a hundred times more for free.

I repeat them my words, again and again

Just in case for a moment the feelings would mould,

I let the thoughts whirl around and suddenly grow

The stuff is not new its terribly old.

I know I know I know.

The strategies are dry and boring

As sorry as my ass on my worst day on grass

Like Wimbledon rain throughout out the touring.

But then there are days I remember

With a smile every now and again,

So there I sit cold as December

Wondering if it will come back and when?

So until the moment the smile lasts a little longer

I will remember one or two things a day,

And hope and hope and hope I will get stronger

Roweena Russell

Unearthed

This small box is mine, I know it well.
I know its internal dimensions, and when
and how I am allowed to leave. I smell
the air; a clever fox must check the scent
and when it's safe she'll go. For when she gets
it wrong, it comes at her with claws and teeth
and even then she can't believe it, even then,
back in the box and breathing hard with fear,
she'll think she made it up and shift the fault,
curl up around it, try to make it fit
as if it could fit. For surely this intent
– *to hang her out to dry, to keep her in it* –
is too fantastic, no true heart this black.
And yet, and yet, she feels him at her back

Natalie Shaw

STAND UP TO BE COUNTED.

Stand up to be counted,

stand up, stand up for your right's

Stand up stand up for the beautiful you,

You were so young, so violated, so badly abused,

But the strong, strong beautiful you,

Stand up, stand up for your rights,

No longer a child, no longer defiled,

But a beautiful women for all mankind to see,

A beautiful women, a strong woman in her own right,

Stand up, stand up to the world, see you can be strong,

Just and honesty, The truth will set you free,

Stand up, stand up for your rights for the just, for the young,

For all of the women in the world,

Who 've been abused, alone in the world.

For your right, just to be heard,

Stand up, stand up for the beautiful women we are,

No more we'll be alone to stand and face our demons,

To account how strong and beautiful we are.

Collectively we fight to be heard,

Just to have justice and be free.

Stand up, stand up for your rights,

Lynda Ann Sherlock

All the beautiful women of this earth.

This poem is about my ex-husband and the domestic violence i went through and my recovery from and still going through.

THE PAST HAS GONE, THIS IS THE FUTURE.

YOU VIOLATED ME SO CRUELY,

YOU,DEGRADED ME SO BADLY,

YOU PLAYED WITH MY HEART MIND AND SOUL,

YOU LAUGHED AND CALLED ME PSYCHO AND LIED TO ALL THAT KNOWS YOU.

YOUR WORDS CAME LIKE A KNIFE TO TRY AND DESTROY ME,

BUT I THROW THEM BACK TO YOU BECAUSE I AM STRONG AND WILL SURVIVE AND LEARN TO LIVE AGAIN.

YOU TRIED TO TAKE AWAY MY LIFE FOR LIFE,

BUT I STAND IN YOUR FACE, GO AND BE NO MORE

BECAUSE I'M SHOWING YOU THE DOOR.

YOU TOOK AWAY MY BEAUTY, MY TRUST AND FAITH IN HUMANITY,

BUT I WILL STAND IN FACE OF VIRTURE AND TRUST AND FAITH AND INHUMANITY AGAIN.

YOUR WORDS FULL OF LIES,

BUT MY WORDS OF TRUTH AND HONESTY "THEY WILL SET ME FREE"

THAT ONE DAY JUSTICE WILL BE SET AND HONESTY WILL BE
LIKE A
BUTTERFLY FREE AND BEAUTY ROLLED IN ONE AND I WILL BE
FULL OF BEAUTY, LOVE AND HONESTY,

NO MORE YOU CAN VIOLATE ME,

NO MORE YOU CAN CALL ME PSYCHO,

NO MORE YOU HAVE THE POWER TO CONTROL ME.

YOU SEE I'M FREE AND WILL ALWAYS BE FREE FROM YOUR
LIES AND HATE BECAUSE I'M JUST ME,

THE TRUTH WILL SET ME FREE.

FREE TO BE A BEAUTIFUL BUTTERFLY AND FLY AWAY TO BE
ME,

NO MORE LIES, NO MORE PAIN,

NO MORE INJUSTICE, BUT BE ME THE REAL STRONG
BEAUTIFUL ME,

A WOMAN FOR ALL TO SEE.

I AM NO MORE ASHAMED, GUILTY AND DIRTY BECAUSE YOU
TOOK AND TOOK AS IF IT WAS YOUR RIGHT

YOU WILL NEVER HAVE MY BODY TO DEVILE, ABUSE, A SHAME

THE TRUTH WILL SET ME FREE.

Lynda Ann Sherlock

Did I do Something Wrong

When he smiles

Celestial bodies whirl

Through personal space

As if I'm clad

In the finest of lace

Dancing to the

Music of the Spheres

But not five minutes later

I again realize all my fears

As the frown

Spreads outward from his face

A can of virtual mace

Sprayed, clogging, dripping

Choking me with my own tears

What occurred during

Those five minutes

Of marital ecstasy?

What sign did he see in me?

Daily he clenches fists

Not reassuring

As clouds cover the stars

Is it something I said?

If so, I wish I was dead

I can never get it right

Or figure out

The discordant song

Did I do something wrong?

Clarissa Simmens

Turkish Train Virgin

My person aboard the train that day,

A tall, dark and creepy man came my way,

But Oh! I was 17 and wasn't it thrilling

That here was this stranger so eloquently spilling;

His admiration for my beauty, my bust,

Give him my number, he said that I must,

And who was I, but a young little girl,

Flattered by this wise, bold man of the world.

Liam, his name, escapes from his lips

And I feel a strange tingle grow forth from my hips

A Man! No! A Stallion!

Has come my way!

And our chance meeting did brighten my day!

His East European background intrigued and enthralled

That late summer evening when he finally called.

We chatted for hours, on love and on friends,

I didn't want this phone call to ever find its end.

But indeed, it did end, as time often does,

And now this young girl was squarely in love

With her Turkish stranger she met on the train,

And soon, it was promised, they would meet again.

'Twas the second of Cember, all twilight and heavy

When i was first told of his friends daring levy,

50 for a virgin, he promised, he swore,

What's more you'll get half!

Who could ask for more!

And so on that night, surrounded by stars,

George Michael's 'Careless Whisper' strummed on guitar,

I found my new being, all lusty and full,

As he bucked and he broncoed just like a bull.

Soon we were comfy, in my first true man

And i often gardened for his Octgenerate nan,

Polishing copper in her floral Mumu,

Thinking that this, was what good girlfriends do.

Our hearts melted open and secrets laid bare,

His best friends tragic death, soon solemnly shared.

I cried for his loss, a heart still so pure,

How was I to know it was simply a lure.

A lie and a promise, so sweetly he broke it,

Now lies were a plenty, whenever he spoke it.

3 months did pass, my blindfold removed

A more discerning decision, I should have behooved.

Yet it was what it was and young hearts were broken

Once all the lies revealed, now that he spoke them.

I moved on and went to dances so gay,

Hoping to never yet ever, come cross his way.

Alas my dear reader, one night, one full moon,

My hopes were not realised, a little too soon.

His face in the moonlight, I dared not it miss,

As he hurled at my person, a full cup of piss.

My shock was in silence, so loud, yet so clear.

I was hastily taken by friends that were near,

And offered some calm in the form of a pipe,

I happily accepted, denial to delight.

And so there it is, the tale of my Virgin,

So hastily taken by a deceitful urchin,

And where might that awful young lad reside now?

In prison, for bomb threats, he spread through the town.

Camilla Strand

What do I do now? (Life after domestic abuse - a glimpse)

Now is the time to grieve

There's no time after you leave

Days are spent

Nights are dreamt

Was this ever meant

To be my life and how

What do I do now?

A life in a war

Secrets behind the door

Another day another bruise

Once again girl you lose

Reeling off a daily put down

Scared to laugh frightened to frown

I began to submit and believe

God give me the strength to leave

Was this ever meant

To be my life and how

What do I do now?

Debby Smith

Stumbling forward

(A poem life after domestic abuse - depression)

The bad things happened year after year

Not seeing the road, is it straight or clear?

Days and nights recollections in a jumble

Cant get out of bed for fear of a stumble

I'm a survivor with some wounds and scars

Looking back its all so alien the life I had on Mars

Today I see the woman I am coming to be

No box of answers with a big gold key

I don't wish to be bright or bold and loud

Scream or shout and stand out in a crowd

Can I just be little old me and not a wanabee

I want to be heard so others can see

Debby Smith

214

Ask Margaret

Men often ask

Why her female

characters

Are so paranoid.

It's not paranoia,

She says,

They just recognise

their situation.

Fi Smith

In Passing

A glass of water.

As it passes your lips

It cleanses, it cools,

Flushes away the dream-thirst

And the doubts

Until all but no memory of it lingers.

The longest sleep begins.

Bruises on the temple fade,

Drugs exit the system,

Abrasions turn to unbroken skin.

You go back to bed

And nothing leaves a mark.

A glass of water.

Down the hatch,

Remnants into the black.

They are eaten away

To almost-nothing,

Concealed deep in your cells.

Fi Smith

This is where I shelter when I shelter

I shelter in clothes several sizes bigger than they should be because I also shelter in too much food.

I shelter in the comfort of carbohydrates that make me feel weak and tired.

But then I can't find shelter from the anger I feel for choosing such destructive cover for my pain.

I shelter in my car when I'm shouting obscenities to those who cut me up or don't feel there is a need to indicate.
I shelter in my writing but no longer shelter my writing as I once did.

I shelter in the writing of others and escape to times not my own.

I find my haven in eighteenth century and rural England;

I walk the path until the land returns to its' former self and I can breath again.

I take cover from the industrial revolution and then find myself sheltering in Gene Hunt's Ford Cortina flying round the streets of early seventies Manchester, knocking down empty boxes to Ballroom Blitz.

But I am not Sam Tyler, I am Sam Taylor and I do not care to shelter from myself.

I always imagined I would shelter in a cottage in the country, with a farmhouse kitchen and stable door where the dogs would sleep on an old sofa and the children's muddy boots would sit upside down on the wellie stand.

I'd wander around barefoot in a floral dress making jam and chutney before saddling up the horses for a ride before dinner.

But the reality is I shelter in a bungalow in the suburbs with a panic button and all round security lighting installed.

The garden is overshadowed by the twelve-foot fences put there for our safety by the Sanctuary Scheme, because the fucker kept breaking in through the allotments at the back of my property.

The windows are alarmed and when the dog barks I wish my son's lightsaber would come to life.

From Monday I will be sheltering in the district of Brighton and Hove, where he is not permitted to enter.

But this shelter makes a prisoner of me and the rest of the country his playground.

At one time I was sent to shelter in a women's refuge, because of the risk he posed.

I was shoved to the back of the cupboard, out of the way because no one knows what else to do.

'Change your identity' they said, 'move away' they said, 'go on the dole' they said.

'It'll be easier on everyone else that way'.

It's all a jolly messy and uncomfortable business all round and as long as it's hidden away, it doesn't exist.

Not on our doorstep!

But there is no sheltering from the regular media reports on the woman who's been knifed to death by her former partner; or the father who killed his children and then himself to get back at the wife who kicked him out.

And we all ask the question, 'why has the system let them down again'?

And I've never been very good at being told to go away and shut up; a silent victim I am not!

So I will continue to emerge from the shelter until somebody listens.

I will climb to the highest tree and insist you know what this man is and I will find sanctuary in the open air.

This morning I sheltered in the words of John Lydon, because it's all bollocks!

Sam Taylor

Sticks and Stones

"Sticks and stones may break my bones,

But words will never hurt me."

Except they did, so many times;

Words that you chose expertly.

Words that made me question just what I meant to you.

A "joke," a jibe that made me wonder what I was meant to do.

A manipulative reminder that you were not to blame.

A twisted grin to emphasise that you enjoyed your game.

A threat, a promise, an order, a sigh.

You whispered "I love you," then tossed me aside.

A cry, a shout, a laugh in the dark.

You cared for yourself, not my broken heart.

Even once I was free, the words kept me chained.

I heard them in my head again and again.

I was fat; I was useless, pathetic and needy.

I'd look in the mirror, but I couldn't see me.

"It's not abuse if he doesn't hit you."

I learned the hard way that that isn't true.

You treated me with such contempt,

Twisting my mind completely...

"Sticks and stones may break my bones"
But words cut just as deeply.

Emma Tofi

Breathe

Every time I see him, my breath tightens

I look at my self in the mirror and I see size 14/16

Safe when large, less attractive to him

Its not so much the touching as the words, the imagery

Nibbling my ear, just writing this is churning up my stomach.

Breathe

Just choosing a name is hard because I still feel as if I am

Betraying him, and family and hurting those I love.

If you had told me then I would have stopped it all.

How do 16 year olds tell adults that whats happening is

happening

When they don't even know its wrong till they are adults

Heard the old saying

If he "raped her" 16 years ago "why is she only coming forward

now"

Anger!!!

It took the girl a heck of a lot of courage to share that

SECRET

Remember the old song

Once I had a Perfect Love by Doris Day

Well I wanted to shout it all from the Hills

Even tell the Golden Daffodils

That I had suffered abuse

Sexual Abuse isn't about touching its

about manipulation.

Being told things, bought things, doing things that

EXCITES THE MALE MEMBER

If it turns him on, makes him "jerk off" .... later alone

then its sexual abuse

I discovered that when I was an adult

Working with kids who had been abused

I had been abused!

I was one of them,

We are Different then

We are always different

Breathe.

Vanessa

Untitled

Fancy being wrapped around an arsehole like you, who stole my youth and my beauty too.

Fancy being wrapped around a big buffoon, it wouldn't have been so bad if you'd danced to my tune

I fed you and clothed you, stroked you and soothed you, still you acted like a mad man and fool.

Black eyes and blood, abuse and misuse you really were a bloody big wuss.
And what did I gain? Oh nothing but pain.

So I'll see you in hell where they'll ring a big bell proclaiming to all that you took a big fall. When I threw you out with a mighty big shout, Over here Mr Officer, he's hiding without.

I jumped on our bed and I drank all your beer, I ate loads of

bacon and now I am queer as I shout to my lover SUE I'M HERE.

Delores William.

Juggler

You, you will not do with your shapes

in the air colouring the sky

two, four, six at a time introducing something

new, like flame. Always fire with you

a show off all elements and higher into

the stars you threw returning to earth transformed

new, us mortals hypnotised by motion,

edged closer. Those shapes

blurred planets whirring satellites. What God were

you, you with the many arms, wrath ablaze

I watched taking my eye off the ball as you threw

planets , shapes, satellites, alight , aloft

and falling backwards did not notice the steel flash

the gun you introduced and steadily drew

too far out I slipped too far out of my own view

Angharad Williams

Owned

I want ink stains on your fingers;

give them here let me see

the blotches of love words written indelibly.

I want your chest to my ear, a conch shell,

your heart beating out a litany of my name.

I want a tattoo on your ass.

Under that constellation of moles;

our initials on a tree.

I want whoever comes after to see

That I set you going; lit

that first expectant spark in your heart's vessels.

Angharad Williams

ON BEING A WIFE

Sweet thing

I see you gazing from your cage

Your folded wings

No longer free to stretch

And glisten in the sunlight

Clipped by promises you made in earnest

No more now to soar above the storm

And hover where the winds of life will take you.

You watch with hollowed eyes

So dull.

Their brightness stripped

The day you lost your freedom

Tied by chains so precious you adore them

And hate yourself for feeling as you do

Yet from your cage you watch

The world go by

And long for freedom

No one ever told you it could be like this

They only spoke of wonder, marvels

Lucky girl!

And you believed!

Jo Wood

DATE RAPE?

"And then he took me."

How she wept, as I, untutored in such horror

Sat and held her while I listened to her pain.

And in that moment-

How I hated all mankind

The male of course.

Their soft and cruel seductions

And their evil warped assumptions

For their power and force directed in this way.

"A film," she sobbed

"That's all he said- I'll take you to the movies

-Just we two."

New jeans so crisp, now just a sad and cruel reminder

Of his coarse and rough mishandling.

"And I cried," she said, "I begged him no

This wasn't how we planned it."

And her sobs grew ever deeper.... aching cries of

Anguish wracked her heaving shaking sobbing form.

"But still he did it-forcing, paining, tearing....."

Tears now flowed afresh in plenty and we clung

Together

Crying for her undeserved disgrace.

Jo Wood

IN MEMORY OF DAYS OF ENDLESS TORMENT

Do you sleep well at night?

Do you ever recall what you did?

What you so nearly did

With your torment

Your lies and abuse?

Do you wonder

what happened

to her who

you so nearly broke

with despair?

Do you care?

Do you ever regret

when your mind becomes clear

for a while?

If it does.

Do you bleed still from wounds

you laid bare?

Do you ever think back?

With remorse

And contrite?

Do you care?

Did you think you would win

She'd give in
She'd succumb
Just play dead
While you played on your game?
And you'd pocket the winnings
and run
Did you honestly think
that you'd win?

Well, you didn't you bastard
She didn't give in
Or succumb
She played dead for a while.
Yes you so nearly won
But she found strength to run
So who won here
I'l let you decide

Jo Wood

THE DRAGONS

By night, the dragons come

With fearsome tails they whip and flick the darkness

into cruel and mean obscenities

that squeal and squeak and groan

with every thrash or blow of unseen plated tails.

And how they wound

Those clawed infected digits, poking, probing, tearing daytime

faith

and hope away, to leave

the three revulsions, grief, despair and loneliness.

The enemy of what I seek

-pure solitude and peace.

Inside my head, they twist each so ambitious thought.

Each ray of hope quashed out

by golden flamed derision

"Who are you?" they roar

"To conquer us

- the demons of your mind?"

The Knot

THE KNOT

The ties that bind

THE KNOT

The bonds of humankind

That fasten each to each

And own to own

Flesh of flesh

And bone of bone

THE KNOT

A Cradle of affection

THE KNOT

A Web of dark protection

A common ground

A peace of mind

The strings that drag us

Gagged and bound

And puppet blind

THE KNOT

Those family ties

A thread of commonsense

A yarn of lies, wrapped in ignorance

THE KNOT

A net of love, a thread of hope

A push and shove

A strangling rope

A tug of war

A cord of harmony

A bolted door

A poisoned tree - a noose

A wedge

A never breaking loose

A double edge

A puzzle

Of love and violence

A muzzle - a falling from the ledge to silence

THE KNOT

Our future in creation

A loop in time

Backbone of our nation

A hidden crime

A noble dream

A fine ideal

A silent scream

A crucible

A melting pot

For what is real and what is...

NOT..

John Woudberg

Contributors

Anonymous likes blogging about feminism, human rights and mental health

Khairani Barokka (b. Jakarta, 1985) is a writer, poet, artist, and disability and arts (self-)advocate. Among her honors, she was an NYU Tisch Departmental Fellow for her masters, Emerging Writers Festival's Inaugural International Writer-In-Residence and Indonesia's first Writer-In-Residence at Vermont Studio Center. Okka is the writer/performer/producer of solo poetry/art show "Eve and Mary Are Having Coffee", which premiered at Edinburgh Fringe 2014. She is currently Artist-In-Residence at Rimbun Dahan, Malaysia. Okka has performed and taught across Asia, the US, Australia, and Europe, and is published in anthologies and literary journals in print and online. She has just completed two full-length poetry manuscripts, "Pilot Light" and "Oil and enamel on linen: poems"; more info at www.khairanibarokka.com / @mailbykite.

Ali Bee (almost her real name) has been a feminist most of her adult life and has been writing women centred songs and stories for about the same length of time. She's a middle aged, disabled, grumpy woman who loves to sing and collects instruments to fill her space, some of which she plays mediocrely, some badly but all of which she enjoys. She gets her idea for her writing from her life, from life in general and sometimes even from Facebook. Her first book of poetry *Trying to Make Sense of Things* is now available.

Catherine Brockhurst is a feminist and a full time working mother, who writes poetry as her own personal form of activism. She has been writing poetry for a few years now and did so after having her son, in some ways as a delayed reaction to the experience. She found herself desperate for a creative outlet and desperate to be heard. The inspiration for a lot of her work are the experiences of women. She write about our lives, our loves, our fears and our hopes. In a world so focused on men she always try to centre my writing on women. She tries to reach out to people with my poems, to show them they are not alone and to express my views in a way that is accessible, meaningful and hopeful.

Cat Brogan won the BBC Edinburgh fringe Poetry Slam. Her poetry has featured on Radio 4, at Latitude Festival and Cheltenham Literary Festival. She has recently finished her MA Writer/Teacher at Goldsmiths and is a full time Spoken Word Educator in a London School. She is originally from Northern Ireland and has performed internationally including Pakistan, Kenya and New York.

Jane Burn is a North East based writer and a member of 52, the North East Women Writing Collective, the Black Light Writing Group and the Tees Women Poets. Her poems have been published in magazines such as Material, The Edge, Butcher's Dog, Ink Sweat & Tears, Nutshells and Nuggets, Alliterati, Lunar Poetry, Stare's Nest, Loch Raven Review and the Black Light Engine Room. She was also long-listed for the Cantebury Poet of the Year Award, the National Poetry Competition and was commended in the Yorkmix 2014. Her work is also featured in Emma Press and Kind of a Hurricane Press Anthologies.

Stephanie Campisi is an Australian-born, Portland-based poet and author whose work has been published in magazines and anthologies worldwide. I've been shortlisted for the Ditmar, Aurealis and Axel Clarke awards. I write silly things at poetdeploriate.tumblr.com and tweet at @readinasitting. 'You Should Be Afraid, He Says' has appeared on I am Not a Silent Poet.

Natalie Collins is a Gender Justice Specialist. She set up Spark (www.sparkequip.org) and works to enable individuals and organisations to prevent and respond to male violence against women. She is also the Creator of DAY (www.dayprogramme.org), an innovative youth domestic abuse and exploitation education programme. She speaks and writes on understanding and ending gender injustice nationally and internationally. She was subjected to abuse by her ex-partner, but has been blessed with a wonderful husband, two excellent children and a glorious life filled with healing and wholeness.

T.J. Collins: As a teacher, T.J. Collins is unable to use her real name in print, due to what school governors have called "uncomfortable questions and possible negative reactions". This sort of shaming and silencing has made her even more determined to speak out and ensure that taboos are challenged in public arenas. As a teacher and writer, Collins has little else to add to a biography, other than marking, planning and sleeping.

El Dia is a radical international poet, doctor of philosophy, and cyberfeminist femmecee. She runs the intersectional radqueerfemmenist blog www.sistersofresistance.org, shares things she fancies at www.eldiadia.com, and tweets @eldiadia.

Oge Ejizu is a University of Surrey graduate with a Bachelors degree in Politics. During her time at University, Oge found a passion for writing, plays and poetry. Inspired by the likes of Katori Hall's 'The Mountaintop' and Shakespeare's 'Othello' and 'Macbeth', Oge uses expressive metaphors to paint a picture through words which will envelope you in the story being told. Oge has produced a number of poems that not only focus on real life issues but are also based on her personal experiences, which makes her body of work relatable and hard hitting. Oge looks forward to learning more about playwriting and the soon release of her play.

Acia Eve: I've worked with victims whose distress has been discredited for well over a decade. Hurt ones who have had to digest their pain and feel it poison their hope for a better tomorrow through no fault of their own. Young women and men who are blamed for the symptoms of this pain, all while their voice as a victim is never heard.

Over the past few years I've been able to witness the power writing has to help these young people tell their story, one not permitted by the narrative of victim blaming.

It reminds me of what writing did for me at their age. And how it has taken me until now to feel like the owner of the copyright for my own tale.

@Extreme_Crochet: "Single parent with three children. I am a survivor of domestic and sexual violence. Hoping to one day make a difference to the women in local area. In the meantime, trying to keep my head above water and give my children the best life possible. My poetry comes from a dark place but helps to bring me some relief from my ptsd."

Rahila Gupta is a freelance journalist, writer and activist. She is a longstanding member of the management committee of Southall Black Sisters and chair of the Nihal Armstrong Trust which funds families of children with cerebral palsy to buy cutting-edge equipment and services. With Kiranjit Ahluwalia she wrote *Provoked,* the story of a battered woman who killed her violent husband and co-wrote the screenplay based on the book, which was released as a film in 2007. Her last book, *'Enslaved'*, on immigration controls, was published in 2007. Her play *Don't Wake Me: The Ballad of Nihal Armstrong* has been nominated for various awards and has been staged in London, Edinburgh, New York and four cities in India. She writes for The Guardian, openDemocracy, New Humanist as well as other journals and websites.

Lynsey Hansford is a mother of three, a professional supporter of women, a writer and a feminist. Find out more about her at www.yourjourneydoula.co.uk or tweet hello @redhairdoula

Barbara Hughes has been involved in politics most of her adult life. She is interested in women's issues, mental health, disability and anti-nuclear campaigns. She is a mother and a grandmother and has been writing about her life in poetry and prose for many years. Hughes used to work in a Rape Crisis Centre and has taken part in many campaigns around domestic violence, pornography, rape and child abuse. She was very active in the peace movement for a long time and loves her cats and Pink Floyd.

Katharina Maria Kalinowski is a poet, writer and translator. She grew up in the North of Germany and moved to the UK in 2011 to study Creative Writing and Drama Studies at De Montfort University in Leicester. Her poems and short stories have previously appeared in the PIYE magazine, Birmingham Review, Demon Crew pamphlet and on the N.A.S.A.-Chandra X-ray Observatory weblog. Katharina lives in Coventry and is currently completing her MA in Writing at the University of Warwick.

Clare Lavery has worked for over 30 years in TESOL/MFL as a teacher trainer, conference speaker, writer and website producer. She worked in ELT publishing sales, research and content editing in the 90s. Lavery's work has taken me worldwide to numerous countries. She lived for 20 years in France, Spain and Italy and is trilingual. She is a freelance creative writer, memoir and poetry writer and lecturer in ESAP in Social Sciences and Law at Northumbria University. Her research interests lie in participatory/biographical research methods in victimology, creativity in research methodology and linguistic human rights issues across borders.

Theresa Lola is poet from London, whose poems speak on a wide range of issues from society to relationships to female empowerment. Her emotional piece 'Bring Back Our Girls' speaking on the Boko Haram kidnapping of the almost 300 girls in Nigeria garnered her international response. In honour of her academic and creative achievements, Theresa was awarded the 'Jack Petchey Outstanding Achievement' award. Her poem 'Do I Deserve the Love of My Mother?' is featured in the anthology 'Essence of love' displayed in The British Library.

Claire Meadows-Haworth: Claire writes poetry to survive. Her poems are a direct response to her abuse and a way of dealing with that abuse. Claire seldom shares her poems because they are so deeply personal, but she new that the EVB book would be a safe place for them. And her hope is that by sharing these words, in some small way she can help other women to survive too.

Claire also writes regularly for her own blog, her work blog, for EVB and other feminist blogs. You can find her on Twitter at @psycho claire.

Huma Munshi is a writer specialising in the areas of gender, race and disability equality. She has a particular interest in raising awareness about violence against women, including honour based violence. She writes regularly for Media Diversified and Open Democracy. A keen theatre and film goer, she often writes reviews on shows. She works in the area of equality law and is a committed trade unionist

Jan Martin is an artist/illustrator, and feminist activist based in Bristol. She has been a professional artist since 1999, and has used her skills for the feminist cause: EVAW & Anti-Slavery graffiti. She has designed for several feminist and women's history exhibitions and projects, as well as illustrations and design for publications, including Bristol Fawcett's 'Cutting Women Out' report, and Bristol Rape Crisis' self-help book. She also runs art/craft sessions at Bristol's One25 drop-in centre, where street sex workers are given help and support.

As well as being a visual artist Martin have always loved to write. She's always written poetry and children's storie, had a couple of articles published online, and contributed a chapter to *The Lightbulb Moment*. Her blog is called Jan Moira's Café.

Victoria M. Massie is a freckled flaneuse wandering the world in search of the little things. She believes in the magic of the minuscule as found in wordplay and her obsession with the double helix. She spends most of her time being an anthropologist.

Claire Moore: Actor, director and co-founder of Certain Curtain Theatre. Established in 1989, Certain Curtain Theatre is a professional touring company whose ground-breaking work has been acclaimed by audiences across the country. Producing exciting, innovative theatre, challenging pre-conceived ideas with dynamic originality... from the page to the stage... Its aim is to provide high-quality, thought-provoking, original theatre for everyone. Certain Curtain Theatre have been at the fore-front of the use of theatre and drama within the field of domestic violence since 1995. Her poem was written for the first #deadwomenwalking march to remember UK women killed by known men – held in London 23rd November 2014

Mary Moylan: I am a writer. Of stories and columns and plays and poems. Since I could read at age 4. Now is my time to explore more of this soul passion. This poem was sparked by a horrible email sent to me yesterday by one of my brothers denouncing me for speaking out about violence in my own family and ordering (!!) me to apologise for speaking out as I would ruin another brother's reputation. Something snapped inside me. The loudest snap yet.

Nicky Phillips lives and writes in rural Hertfordshire. Her poems have appeared recently in *Brittle Star* and *South Bank Poetry*, and online on *Nutshells and Nuggets* and *The Lake*.

Anthologies where you can find her poems include *'Heart Shoots', an Anthology in aid of Macmillan Cancer Support* (Indigo Dreams Publishing, 2013), and *The Book of Love and Loss* (Belgrave Press, 2014).

Mary Rugman: I'm an English teacher and survivor. I went to Ruskin College, Oxford in my early twenties and studied English and Creative Writing while exiting an abusive relationship. Encouraged to apply for Higher Education, I decided to aim for a career in teaching the subject I love. After years of studying, training and working as a single mum, my life was thrown into turmoil when I was drugged and raped. I have raised money for local centres offering support for victims of sexual violence and I have hope. Hope for better justice for survivors of male violence and an end to rape culture.

Lynn Schreiber: Lynn Schreiber In 2014, Lynn launched Jump! Books, to publish fiction and non-fiction books for kids, including the 12Women series, highlighting the achievements and legacies of forgotten women of history.

Natalie Shaw lives and works in London. Her poetry has appeared in a number of online and print journals, including Butcher's Dog, Prole and Ink, Sweat & Tears.

Lynda Anne Sherlock is a 47 old women and a mother of two children. She is doing a p/t degree in fine art and would love to go into teaching with others who have disabilities. She has had mental health and physical difficulties and has had for a long time. She was also abused as a child as well as suffering with domestic violence for my ex-husband who she lived with for 16 :years . They are now divorced. She is interested in politics, sociology, social policy. She loves all different kinds of art but loves art history. She play the piano and loves cooking, sewing, writing poems and short stories. She also likes all kinds of music and loves watching films and documentaries. Her motto is never give up and keep trying even when things get tough.

Clarissa Simmens is an independent poet (since the age of four) and a Romani drabarni (Gypsy herbalist/adviser). She is also a music addict, and writes her poetry simply, striving to compose musically: talking blues, folktales, memoirs of life; all types of genres mainly in a Minor Key. She hopes to heal souls and maybe poetry can accomplish that. Simmens has a number of poetry books published on kindle: *Maiden, Mother and Mage: A Day of Poetry, Poetic Alchemy (Talking Blues)* and *Poetry of Memory (Six Decades from the Space-Time Continuum).* You can also find her work on her blog Poeturja

Debby Smith: Writer and poet, loves to write comedy.

Camilla Strand: Camilla Strand is an Australian second wave feminist, artist and author of the women's movie blog www.SheilaMedia.com

Fi Smith is a journalist from Dublin, working for Craic-it.com, a site for Irish expats in London, and the First Fortnight mental health awareness festival (firstfortnight.com) - Twitter: @fifilebon

Emma Tofi is an author and blogger, living in Cornwall who spends her free time co-running the Fifty Shades Is Domestic Abuse campaign.

Delores William When I was 16 years old my parents left the country and left my brother and I to our own fate. I met a man and for the next 5 years he beat me up nearly every single day I had 2 children but our life was hell. He stole my money and in the end I had one of my children adopted. On my 21st birthday I decided to leave him. It was the best thing I ever did. It wasn't easy though but I stayed strong and never went back to the hateful man. I went on to have another child Richie 7 years later who was brought up in an atmosphere of love and I was able to be the loving mother I was meant to be. Unfortunately poor Richie was killed in an accident 12 years later. I thought I would die but I didn't I lived. To make some sense of my life I returned to education gained a masters degree and became a journalist. I now work for a social media company and sometimes wonder how far I have come. Writing this has brought a tear to my eye. But I'm proud of what I have become.

Angharad Williams lives, writes and drinks too much coffee in Manchester. Her poetry has appeared previously online and in print and she is slowly working towards speaking out about the violence that she, and too many other women endure.

John Woudberg : Childhood survivor, writer and co-founder of Certain Curtain Theatre Company. Established in 1989, Certain Curtain Theatre is a professional touring company whose ground-breaking work has been acclaimed by audiences across the country. Producing exciting, innovative theatre, challenging pre-conceived ideas with dynamic originality... from the page to the stage... Its aim is to provide high-quality, thought-provoking, original theatre for everyone. Certain Curtain Theatre have been at the fore-front of the use of theatre and drama within the field of domestic violence since 1995. His poem is taken from their award-winning domestic violence drama *THE KNOT*

www.ingramcontent.com/pod-product-compliance
Lightning Source LLC
Chambersburg PA
CBHW070804050426
42452CB00011B/1891